Handbook for

CANTORS

REVISED EDITION

Handbook for
CANTORS

REVISED EDITION

Diana Kodner

LITURGY
TRAINING
PUBLICATIONS

Gabe Huck was the editor of this book. Michael
Hay read the manuscript and offered many
helpful comments. Audrey Novak Riley was the
production editor. The design is by Lisa Buckley
and the book was set in Bembo by Mark
Hollopeter, the production artist. Musical
notation was set by Marc Southard. Printed
by Bawden Printing in Eldridge, Iowa.

Cover photos: Musical staves, I. Burman/
P. Boorman, © Tony Stone Images; Singer,
© Antonio Pérez.

Music acknowledgments begin on page 113.

Library of Congress catalog card number
97-71919

ISBN 1-56854-097-3
HBCANR

01 00 99 98   5 4 3 2 1

Acknowledgments

Contents

Examples,
Illustrations and
Exercises

Definitions of Terms

ACCENT
to emphasize or give prominence over other non-accented notes or syllables

ACCLAMATIONS
affirmations of praise and assent, for example, the gospel acclamation and acclamations to the eucharistic prayer

ADVENT
the first season of each liturgical year, beginning on the fourth Sunday before Christmas, recalling the anticipation of the birth of Christ and looking toward his second coming

AMBO
the lectern or pulpit used for the proclamation of the word

ANIMATOR
one who initiates or encourages movement or activity, or in the case of the liturgy, the participation of the assembly

ASPIRATING A VOWEL
to pronounce with the addition of an initial vocal sound or noise

CHANT
to sing; or the song itself, frequently unmeasured and with multiple syllables sung on certain predominant pitches

CHRISTMASTIME
the festive season from December 25 (and its vigil) through the feast of the Baptism of the Lord

COLLECT
a prayer by the presider that concludes the introductory rite at liturgy

CREED
a statement of religious beliefs; part of the ordinary of the Mass, that is, a part of the Mass that does not vary from day to day or season to season

DECAY
the gradual decline in loudness or volume of a tone as it reverberates

DOUBLE BARS
two vertical lines separating sections of a printed musical composition

DOWNBEAT
the first beat of a measure, usually the principally accented pulse

DYNAMICS
variations in volume or loudness, for example, *forte* (loud), *piano* (soft)

EASTERTIME
the great Fifty Days, a festive season that begins with the Easter Vigil on Holy Saturday and concludes with the feast of Pentecost

EUCHARIST
literally, "thanksgiving"; refers to the Mass in general and the liturgy of the eucharist within the Mass, as well as to the consecrated bread and wine

FIFTH
a musical interval of five degrees of a diatonic scale

FOURTH
a musical interval of four degrees of a diatonic scale

GENERAL INTERCESSIONS

the petitions or prayers of the faithful made to God for the needs of the church, the world, the afflicted, the local community, those assembled and the dead

GLORIA

the hymn of praise that follows the penitential rite in the liturgy; part of the ordinary of the Mass (omitted in Advent and Lent)

GLOTTAL ATTACK

the explosive opening of the glottis at the beginning of a tone, owing to the build-up of air behind the glottis prior to phonation

HALF-STEP

a musical interval equal to one-twelfth of an octave

HOMILY

a short sermon or religious discourse on the scriptures

INITIATING A TONE

to begin singing; to phonate

INTERCESSION

petition or prayer requesting favors for another; at liturgy, one of the prayers of the faithful directed toward God

INTERVAL

the distance between tones; the difference in pitch

INTONATION

tuning; the matching of tones or the calculation of distance between tones

INTONE

to utter something in musical tones; or the initial statement of a musical idea (to be repeated by the assembly)

LECTOR

one who proclaims the word of God at liturgy; a reader

LEGATO

smooth, connected movement from one tone to another

LENT

the penitential season from Ash Wednesday up to but not including the liturgy of Holy Thursday

LIGHT VOICE

a voice with fewer overtones and less volume than others

LITURGY OF THE HOURS

a prescribed form of worship including psalms, hymns, prayers and scripture, to be celebrated at stated times of the day, such as Morning Prayer or Evening Prayer

LITURGY OF THE EUCHARIST

the second major part of the Mass, consisting primarily of the communion rite

LITURGY OF THE WORD

the first major part of the Mass, consisting primarily of readings from scripture

MAJOR THIRD

a musical interval of three degrees of a diatonic scale or four half-steps

MASSES WITH CHILDREN

the official Vatican document, the *Directory for Masses with Children,* makes special liturgical suggestions and allowances for such gatherings, for instance, specific additional acclamations to the eucharistic prayer

MELODIC RANGE

the distance from the lowest to the highest note in a musical passage

METER

the rhythmic organization of a piece or section; the number of beats per measure and the note that designates one beat

METRONOME

a device that marks the beat with a regular repeated tick or flash of light; it calculates the number of beats per minute

MINISTRY

service of God in the service of others

MINOR THIRD

a musical interval of three half-steps

MUSICAL MOTIVE

a recurrent phrase or combination of notes

MUSICAL PHRASE

a complete musical sentence or thought

ORDINARY TIME

that part of the year not included in Advent, Christmastime, Lent, or Eastertime; more than half the year; *ordinary* is related to *ordered*, therefore, counted; the Sundays of Ordinary Time are numbered, as the Fifth Sunday of Ordinary Time

PASTORAL

relating to the spiritual care and guidance of a community

PITCH

a musical tone of specific frequency (the number of sound waves per second); high notes have many rapid waves per second or high frequency

PREPARATION OF THE GIFTS

formerly called the offertory, it is the procession with the gifts and preparation of the eucharistic table; it separates the liturgy of the word from the liturgy of the eucharist

PRESIDER

the one who exercises guidance and direction of a liturgical gathering; at Mass, the priest is the presider, since he is the only one authorized to preside over the eucharist

PROCESSION

a group of people moving in an orderly, ceremonial way; the liturgy usually has an opening procession, gospel procession, procession with the gifts, communion procession and closing procession

PROJECTION

making oneself heard clearly

RANGE

all the pitches within the capacity of a voice

REGISTER

a division within the range of a voice; there are typically three — chest, middle and head voice or falsetto

RELEASING A TONE

the act of concluding a note

REPERTOIRE

the list of compositions a musician is prepared to perform

REVERBERATION

the reflection of sound from various surfaces, and the consequent continuation of that sound

ROSARY

a traditional Roman Catholic devotion consisting of meditation on five sacred mysteries during the recitation of five decades (groups of ten) of Hail Marys, each of which begins with an Our Father and ends with a Glory to the Father; also refers to the set of beads often used with this devotion

RUBRICS

liturgical directives found in the sacramentary, the lectionary and other ritual books, originally printed in red, hence the name

SCHOLA

traditionally, the choir of a monastery or cathedral

SECOND VATICAN COUNCIL
the 21st ecumenical council (1962 – 65) of the Catholic Church, called by Pope John the 23rd; the decrees of Vatican II resulted in many changes in the life of the church, such as the use of vernacular language instead of Latin at liturgy, the call for the full, conscious and active participation of the assembly in the liturgy and the restoration of the role of the cantor, among others

SEVENTH
a musical interval of seven degrees of a diatonic scale

SIXTH
a musical interval of six degrees of a diatonic scale

STACCATO
short, disconnected articulation of notes

STRAIGHT TONE
sung without vibrato

TEMPO
the speed of a piece as related to the meter

TONAL CENTER
the pitch around which all tones and harmonies are organized in a particular composition

TONE QUALITY
timbre or musical "color"

TRIDUUM
the three days which are the pinnacle of the liturgical year — Holy Thursday, Good Friday and the Easter Vigil

VIBRATO
slight, rapid, regular variation in pitch used in singing and in the playing of many musical instruments

VOCAL QUALITY
timbre or "color" of a voice

VOCALIZATION
phonation; the production of vocal sound; specifically, exercising or warming up the voice

VOLUME
loudness or softness

WASHING OF FEET
the Mandatum; the ritual action of Jesus at the Last Supper and hence, the ritual of the Catholic community on Holy Thursday

WHOLE STEP
two half-steps; the interval from the first tone of a diatonic scale to the second

Foreword

I want to begin this revised edition of *Handbook for Cantors* with some background on myself and the context in which this book was written.

I am a divorced woman of 39. I was raised a non-practicing Jew and a sometimes Unitarian. My mother is a violinist and my father was an artist, so art and music have always been part of my life. As an adult I went through the catechumenate, and I was baptized and received into the church at the Easter Vigil in 1981. My first experience of conversion to the faith — my leap from intellectual curiosity to real belief — was profound. It has made me pursue my faith and my ministry with great fervor. It has also caused me to struggle with issues of the exclusion of women or the disenfranchisement of the divorced — some human aspects of church. Even so, I believe what I believed fifteen years ago, I am still deeply touched by faith and I continue to cherish belonging to the body of Christ.

This book is my gift of gratitude for all this — for beauty and music and art and God and God's people. There is no way I could thank everyone by name, but I need to highlight some of those who have most influenced my work. I was blessed from the start with extraordinary teachers and mentors: Bob Oldershaw, Bob Batastini, Dorothy Dwight, Robert Harris and Gabe Huck. Gabe is the one who encouraged me to write this book, and who continues to encourage me to do wonderful things. Other influences have come from brilliant colleagues like Mike Hay (who once again read this manuscript) and Mary Beth Kunde-Anderson. My greatest debt, however, is to those I have been graced to serve: the people of Queen of All Saints Parish in Chicago, St. Patrick Parish in Lake Forest, Our Lady of Perpetual Help in Glenview, St. Nicholas in Evanston, and currently, Sacred Heart in Winnetka. I continue to be taught, stirred and humbled by this wonderful ministry.

Diana Kodner

The Cantor

When the first edition of this book was published in 1988, the word "cantor" was still unfamiliar to many Catholics. Now, thanks to the work of parish music ministers and liturgists, diocesan offices of worship, educators and publishers, the term is fairly commonplace. The role of the cantor continues to evolve, however; there is disagreement and, I would argue, misunderstanding about the function and purpose of the cantor. In these pages I will attempt to present an informed point of view, one to which I am committed.

Two basic schools of cantoring have evolved. One is based on the French "animateur" or animator, and the other is perhaps more closely related to a Jewish model. In Jewish worship, the cantor is the singer of holy songs who offers prayers to God on behalf of the community. The Jewish cantor is seldom an animator of the assembly's singing, but is rather an interpreter of the assembly's spirit, singing and praying on behalf of the assembly.

However, if we were to import this model into Roman Catholic worship without adaptation, we would be misunderstanding its significance for the Jews and its applicability to post–Vatican II Roman Catholic liturgical celebration.

Not much is known about the role of the cantor in the early church. We do know that as the church became institutionalized in the third century, so did various liturgical roles, including that of the cantor. The cantor was a member of the assembly and part of the schola who would chant certain portions of the liturgy, such as the psalms or alleluias. As scholas and then choirs developed, they took over the role of the cantor, and eventually the singing of the assembly. The cantor disappeared. Song, which had been integral to the liturgy, finally was heard only at "high" Masses. Even then, the choir sang and the assembly listened.

The reforms of the Second Vatican Council restored the role of the cantor to Roman Catholic liturgical practice. The people were to assemble as full, conscious and active participants in the liturgy. To this end, song leaders were used to encourage the participation of the assembly for some time after the Council. Often this encouragement was simply the announcing of page numbers, and then the singing of the people's parts into a microphone. Sometimes the song leader would "conduct" the assembly with big, swirling gestures.

Time has proven, however, that this kind of encouragement is very limited. While the visible participation of liturgical ministers in sung worship is encouraging to the assembly, it is usually the organ or other instruments that actually leads song. The amplification of a single voice over the singing of the assembly is generally a deterrent to their full and active participation. Extraneous gestures are not only superfluous but also distracting — and frequently annoying. Anything that calls attention to itself is to be avoided. To paraphrase Brother Robert of the French Taizé community, liturgical music should be like John the Baptist, pointing the way to the Lord and never to itself.

At the same time, there are those who can use conducting gestures to foster the assembly's singing, and who can use the gentle sound of their unaccompanied voices to invite the people into the song. Such skillful leaders thus invite the assembly not merely to sing along, but to intimately partake of the unique mystery and beauty of each song of praise or lament. John Bell of the Iona Community in Scotland and Dr. Alice Parker are masters of this type of song leading, which is not easily imitated. Deceptively simple, it requires a high level of musical craft and a great deal of practice. Leaders like these seem to disappear, like the Cheshire cat in *Alice in Wonderland,* leaving only the song. "Song Leading Revisited," beginning on page 87, is devoted to this style of cantoring or song leading, which takes our ministry forward. Beyond eliciting full and active participation, and beyond modeling appropriate interpretation, cantors and song leaders can deepen the experience of worship by encouraging a genuine response from the assembly. Its goal is to allow those assembled to give expression to what is inside them, not to reflect what is inside the cantor.

The *General Instruction of the Roman Missal* is the principal post-conciliar description of the way we are to celebrate Mass. (It is printed in the front of the sacramentary, the book that contains the order of service and prayers for the Mass.) The *General Instruction* offers several ways that the cantor serves in the liturgy:

> There should be a cantor or choirmaster to direct and encourage the people in singing. If there is no choir, the cantor leads the various songs, and the people take their own part. (#64)

> The chanter of the psalms is to sing the psalm or other biblical song between the readings. The cantor should be trained in the art of singing psalms and be able to speak clearly and distinctly. (#67)

The role of cantor has come to include a number of things. It is generally considered the ministry of the cantor to:

- lead moments of worship with solo song
- share in proclaiming the word of God, particularly as psalmist in the liturgy of the word
- teach the assembly its songs, refrains and acclamations and
- animate the sung worship of the assembly.

The cantor is a member of the assembly who serves the assembly in its worship. The cantor must be clearly identifiable as someone connected to those gathered and to the entire experience of worship that they share. Usually, this precludes an outsider, someone not of the community or not of the faith. Sometimes, however, an outsider is quite able to identify with the assembly. And there are many transient gatherings that bring together people who do not otherwise form a community. In such cases, it is the cantor's accessibility rather than the cantor's familiarity that is essential. However, I have come to believe that this ministry calls for a fully initiated member of the Catholic church.

The charism of the cantor is to act as a catalyst for the sung expression of faith within the assembly. While solo song is the cantor's most obvious vehicle for this, there are nonmusical ways in which a cantor must be able to communicate and to animate.

This ministry requires a great deal of competence, but it is not the same competence as that of the entertainer or showperson. The cantor must be singer, proclaimer, liturgical minister and spiritual leader, a singer of lullabyes and victory songs, a true story-teller and a person of prayer, highly attuned to the meaning of a moment and to the meanings of things and gestures.

How to Use This Book with a Group

A group seeking to use this book should schedule weekly sessions for at least four weeks. Determine assigned reading for each session, gradually working through this book. Feel free to include additional reference materials.

Each session might begin with a reflective exercise such as the one suggested on page 21, and with communal prayer such as a simple form of evening prayer.

Allow time at each session for group discussion of the previously assigned reading.

Some time should be spent on group vocal warm-up and on vocal exercises from the chapter "The Cantor as a Singer." Then the remainder of each session should be spent applying what has been learned from the reading and exercises to cantorial rendition. Each member of the group should have an opportunity to sing (and perhaps to teach) a psalm, litany or song. The repertoire need not be limited to what is familiar, but should be chosen considering the needs and abilities of the group.

A leader or the other group members should then offer constructive input for each participant. This could be vocal instruction, reaction to the person as a cantor, and even words of encouragement!

One point from this book that should be emphasized is that the excessive use of the cantor — cantor dominance of the assembly's singing — must be avoided. This point bears repetition in the training sessions.

Another area of great concern is the need for preparation. Begin with how the cantors have prepared for these sessions. Are they ready? Have they prepared reading assignments? Have they prepared to sing for one another? Are they punctual? If the answer to any of these questions is no, make sure that this area is addressed.

The last session might be a time for reflection, giving participants a chance to share thoughts and impressions of the training they have shared, and to reflect upon their parish ministry.

The purpose of this book is to help cantors understand their craft and, beyond developing proficiency, to "become" cantors. "How-to's" are important, but they can lead one to stand outside the experience in a mode of unending analysis. Ultimately, the how-to's should free us to forget them. Only then can we stand unprotected and transparent before and within the assembly.

This book is only a resource, although one to which the cantor can return again and again. Only experience will teach everything that is needed. Not everything here is for the beginner; much will be challenging even to the experienced cantor. This book may be used by a group working together or by an individual. A number of dioceses have used the first edition of this book in their cantor schools. The person using the book alone should understand that it is often helpful to have the input of others when one is practicing an art that involves communication.

The sections of this book are overlapping and interdependent areas offering points of departure for discussion and study. Scattered throughout the book are practical recommendations, exercises and reference materials to support the information provided. Many of these are set apart in boxes for easy reference. The chapter "Spirituality," which begins on page 109, offers suggestions for the cantor's growth in prayer.

If cantors are to be effective in their ministry, they need to understand their role and its place in liturgical celebration. These are always evolving. Cantors need to understand their voices and so avoid and overcome flaws that detract from the expression of texts. They need to practice their ministry until it is fully a part of them and then nurture what has been acquired. Such an approach will make this a joyful ministry for cantors and for those they serve.

FURTHER READING: CANTORS

Michael Connolly, *The Parish Cantor: Helping Catholics Pray in Song* (Chicago: GIA Publications, Inc. 1981, 1991).

Joseph Gelineau, *Voices and Instruments in Christian Worship: Principles, Laws and Applications,* translated by Clifford Howell (Collegeville MN: The Liturgical Press, 1985).

James Hansen, *The Ministry of the Cantor* (Collegeville MN: The Liturgical Press, 1985).

Gabe Huck, *How Can I Keep from Singing?* (Chicago: Liturgy Training Publications, 1989).

Lawrence J. Johnson, *The Mystery of Faith: The Ministers of Music* (Washington: National Association of Pastoral Musicians, 1983). Pages 37–44.

The Milwaukee Symposia for Church Composers: A Ten-Year Report (Chicago: Liturgy Training Publications, 1992).

Alice Parker, *Melodious Accord* (Chicago: Liturgy Training Publications, 1991).

The Eucharistic Liturgy

The eucharistic liturgy, the Mass, is the celebration cantors will participate in most frequently. Every liturgy is different in some ways, but all Masses follow a certain basic form. Music is an integral part of the Sunday liturgy.

The Introductory Rite

The introductory rite of the liturgy always includes the sign of the cross, the greeting and the opening prayer. The introductory rite may also include a gathering song, the blessing and sprinkling of water or a penitential rite, and the Gloria (outside of Advent and Lent). These elements work together to prepare the assembly, as a community, to hear the word and to celebrate the eucharist. The whole introductory rite should have a flow and pacing that goes beyond a succession of rubrics. Music should be an integral element of the introductory rite and not a decorative addition to it.

As with any musical moment in the liturgy, the cantor's role for an opening hymn or gathering song will depend upon several things. Does the song need to be announced? Is this piece sung in its entirety by the assembly? If so, the cantor may not be required to do anything. Might this song or hymn require special animation of the assembly? Does the song or hymn have musical passages that require a cantor? There is a tendency to overuse the cantor, or to use the cantor in ways that do little to enhance the role of the assembly. As a rule of thumb, the cantor should only do what is needed and no more.

After the opening hymn or gathering song, you need only be prominent for pieces requiring special animation or the rendering of solo passages. These might include the litany of the penitential rite or a setting of the Gloria sung in alternation between choir and assembly or cantor and assembly. There might also be a song for the sprinkling rite, which sometimes replaces the penitential rite. Many recent compositions for the sprinkling rite need a cantor.

Care should be taken in selecting music for the introductory rite. Music is essential, but failure to understand and respect the nature of the introductory rite can sometimes lead to overload: too much unrelated music, or just too much music. The whole movement of the liturgy to the end of the opening prayer should be clear and unified.

The Liturgy of the Word

The liturgy of the word requires careful timing and pacing. It usually comprises:

- reading from the Hebrew Scriptures
- psalm
- reading from the letters of the New Testament
- gospel acclamation
- reading from the gospels
- homily
- creed
- prayer of intercession

During the readings, your full attention should be on the lector. You should be able to recall the readings after the liturgy. (Worrying about the psalm during the first reading will not make it any better.) When the lector has finished, wait before beginning the psalm. Allow time for the lector to be seated and allow more time for reflective silence.

A period of silence is called for after each of the first two readings. Your parish probably has some standard way to carry this out. In many cases it will be for you to determine the length of the silence. Cantors should agree on the length of this silence so all can relax into the silence and absorb the word they have heard. You must be quiet and still during this period. If you fidget or glance at your watch, you will encourage impatience and discomfort.

Then move deliberately, without haste, to the place from which you will sing. The instrumentalist should not begin the psalm until you are ready. It is appropriate to sing the psalm from the ambo, since this helps people to understand that the psalm is also the word of the Lord, but it is not essential. Logistics of place and movement must be taken into consideration.

The most common musical rendition of the responsorial psalm begins with an instrumental statement of the refrain, an intonation by the cantor, and its repetition by the entire assembly. Only rarely, and for very good reasons, should you deviate from this practice. It is not a good idea to use the first half of a refrain as the intonation, unless the second half is identical in every way. All of the psalm verses given in the lectionary should be sung. These are often not the entire psalm, but selected verses for liturgical use. There may be a doxology stanza (Father, Son and Spirit) provided, but this is intended to be used in the Liturgy of the Hours. Omit it for Mass. When you have finished the psalm and the accompaniment has ended, wait a moment and then return to your place. Do not hurry, but move calmly and deliberately.

The same inclusion of silence applies to the timing of the gospel acclamation. Allow the agreed-upon pause after the second reading before moving into your position. In some parishes, your cue comes from the presider or the instrumentalist. All should be clear about the length of the silence and the cue for the acclamation. It will not usually be necessary, but if it is clear that the assembly is remaining seated, you should gesture for them to stand. As soon as the gospel acclamation has concluded, perhaps even earlier, direct your attention to the book and the gospel reader. Listen attentively to this proclamation of the word. Your only purpose at this moment is to listen.

In both the psalm refrain and the assembly's alleluia, remember to move back from the microphone so your amplified voice will not be heard over the voices of the assembly.

Leave your music where it is until the gospel reading has concluded and it is time for all to be seated. Then the action of the entire assembly will cover any movement you need to make. Just as you were during the readings, be attentive to the homily.

Do not compete with the presider or the assembly in the recitation of the creed, or any other recitation in the liturgy. These are intended to be spoken in unison by the entire assembly. While cantors and other liturgical ministers should enthusiastically participate, they must be careful not to overbalance the assembly. Their voices should not be picked up by the microphone and amplified.

The general intercessions can and often should be sung. Those who write the prayers need to ensure that they are not too wordy. Pacing is important. These prayers should have a sense of urgency, and the assembly's response should flow from the intercessions. An overlap between the leader's invitation and the assembly's response can be very effective.

The Liturgy of the Eucharist

The liturgy of the eucharist begins with the preparation of the gifts and continues through the eucharistic prayer and the communion rite. The communion rite comprises the Lord's Prayer, the sign of peace, the "Lamb of God" litany, the communion procession, a time of silence and the prayer after communion. Lesser elements, such as the Lord's Prayer, should not overshadow the eucharistic prayer and its acclamations.

The preparation of the gifts is not an ideal time for singing by the assembly, as there is already considerable activity taking place. In addition to the preparation of the gifts, the collection is taken. It often complicates matters to attempt a hymn or song. Instrumental music can help the assembly rest a little among all the words that are necessary to the liturgy. Besides, this is meant to be a lesser moment in the liturgy.

After the preparation of the gifts, the liturgy of the eucharist continues with the eucharistic prayer, which is the core of the entire liturgy. You should be attentive and participatory during the eucharistic prayer, but it is neither necessary nor helpful for you to stand at the microphone. Respond as a member of the assembly when the presider leads the preface dialogue. Even if this is sung, it should not be necessary for you to lead the assembly's responses; your presence and amplified voice will only distract from the liturgical focus.

The assembly's acclamations to the eucharistic prayer are usually the "Holy, holy," the memorial acclamation and the great "Amen." (There are some through-composed settings of the eucharistic prayer punctuated by numerous acclamations. These are generally based on the model of the eucharistic prayers for Masses with children.) If the musical setting is familiar to the assembly and

---

Cantor Commandments

- Be attentive to the liturgy.
- Never steal the focus from others.
- Lead with authority.
- Listen for the singing of the assembly.
- Participate fully and enthusiastically.

not changed too often, the assembly will sing the acclamations with confidence.

If the cantors at your parish have been singing the acclamations into a microphone for some time, allow ample time for a successful change. If, after several weeks, the assembly is still not responsive, consider what the source of the problem might be. Is the instrumental leadership adequate? Is the tempo steady and well-suited to the setting? Are the instruments loud enough? Are they too loud? Are the presider and other liturgical ministers participating? Are the musical settings too difficult? Is the key too high? Are the tunes stale or trite? Is the room so poor acoustically that it is not possible to hear the singing of the assembly, or for them to hear each other?

The Our Father may be sung, but the setting should be accessible to all and should not be out of proportion to this liturgical moment. (The Malotte setting of the Lord's Prayer is not a good choice.) A song is not called for during the sign of peace. An exception might be made from time to time, but this should not become a regular practice. The risk in highlighting these lesser liturgical moments is that the most significant points in the liturgy will be diminished. Everything in the communion rite should lead to the communion procession.

The "Lamb of God" litany should be sung. It begins as the presider starts to break the bread and should last until the breaking of the bread and the preparation of the wine are completed, and the presider is ready to begin the invitation: "This is the Lamb of God . . ." This litany can be especially effective if linked instrumentally to the communion song. It is most important that the communion song begin promptly after the people's response, "Lord, I am not worthy . . ." If the song does not begin until after the priest has received communion, his action is separated and distanced from the communion of the assembly. The assembly can also turn inward during the pause, if the song does not begin immediately.

The very nature of the communion procession calls for song by the assembly. It is most practical to use a setting with a refrain. This enables people to sing without carrying music sheets or hymnals. The cantor should not feel intrusive or be reluctant to lead. Now is the time for people to be aware of those around them, to be aware of the church here nourished at the common table by the body and blood of Christ. Song is an integral part of our communion: It is a natural accompaniment to the procession, an audible presence of brothers and sisters to one another, a source of insight into the mystery in which we share. During communion, some will be waiting to receive communion, some will be focused on the words of the eucharistic ministers and some will already have received communion. The action of the whole can be unified by a single, well-chosen communion song. The communion song may be extended by instrumental verses, by repeating the refrain each time it is sung or by simple repetition of earlier verses.

Only rarely should more than one song be used for the communion procession. That means that each parish needs a repertoire of six to ten strong pieces to use — so strong that any one of them can only be more loved if it is sung all through the ten or fifteen minutes of communion. If two songs are ever needed, they could be woven together in some musical way. At the very least they should be musically and textually compatible. Two very different styles of music may work together well depending on key and melodic content. The two songs on this page and the next illustrate this.

Refrain

We re-mem-ber how you loved us to your death, and still we cel-e-brate, for you are with us here; And we be-lieve that we will see you when you come, in your glo-ry, Lord, we re-mem-ber, we cel-e-brate, we be-lieve.

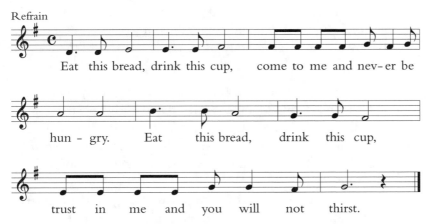

Refrain

Eat this bread, drink this cup, come to me and nev-er be hun - gry. Eat this bread, drink this cup, trust in me and you will not thirst.

People are much more likely to participate in the communion song when it can be sung without books or music. The song should also be something that wears well over the period of communion, and over a number of weeks. A dozen such pieces could suffice as repertoire for any community. The song should ideally begin when the first person receives communion (even when this is the priest) and should not end until the ritual action has ended.

The text of the communion song need not be explicitly about holy communion. Texts emphasizing the communal nature of the action are preferable to private devotional pieces.

Psalmody can be a good choice here, and one that is seldom explored. If you have used the psalm of the day in the liturgy of the word, a seasonal psalm could be used at communion, or vice versa. There are a number of pieces from the music of Taizé that are very effective either as ostinatos or as refrains alternated with verses. These include "Ubi Caritas," "Confitemini Domino," "Jesus, Remember Me" and "In the Lord I'll Be Ever Thankful." The traditional chant "Ubi Caritas" is also appropriate. In the contemporary genre, "You Are All We Have" by Francis Patrick O'Brien and "God Is Love" by David Haas are good choices. Suzanne Toolan's "Jesus Christ, Yesterday, Today and Forever," which is reminiscent of the Taizé music, is a newer piece that works well at communion.

Music in Catholic Worship, a guideline prepared by the United States Bishops' Committee on the Liturgy, is very specific about the communion song.

The communion song should foster a sense of unity. It should be simple and not demand great effort. It gives expression to the joy of unity in the body of Christ and the fulfillment of the mystery being celebrated. (#62)

After communion it is possible to have a song or hymn of thanksgiving, or one of a more reflective nature. This may or may not involve the cantor. Examine your reasoning before adding a song at this point. Will this music contribute significantly to the community's celebration, or will it merely satisfy some special interest?

The communion rite and the complete liturgy of the eucharist conclude with the prayer after communion, which is spoken or sung by the presider.

The Concluding Rite

The liturgy concludes with the blessing and dismissal. If a closing song is sung, it is preferable that all the ministers, including the presider, remain in place and sing at least some of the song. Do not expect the assembly to stay and sing after the liturgical ministers have left. If there is a formal procession, music should accompany the movement. If the hymn is not long enough, the music can be extended instrumentally.

If the hymn requires no solo singing on your part, you may process with the other ministers or you may remain as a part of the assembly. When the liturgy is over, you may want to linger a little. Often, people who are unfamiliar to you will feel that they know you through the liturgy. Some will have comments, positive or negative, that may be useful to you, other musicians or other liturgical ministers.

FURTHER READING: LITURGY

The Liturgy Documents: A Parish Resource, edited by Elizabeth Hoffman (Chicago: Liturgy Training Publications, 1991). The most significant liturgy documents of the church.

Austin Fleming, *Preparing for Liturgy* (Chicago: Liturgy Training Publications, 1997). Emphasizes the preparation of liturgy as opposed to "planning."

Gabe Huck, *Liturgy with Style and Grace* (Chicago: Liturgy Training Publications, 1984). Basic guide to liturgical celebration: liturgical ministers, the liturgical year, components of the eucharistic liturgy.

Gabe Huck et al., *Preaching About the Mass* (Chicago: Liturgy Training Publications, 1992). Sample homilies and accompanying pieces for parish bulletins explore why we gather, listen, intercede, give thanks and praise, and eat and drink together.

Gabe Huck, editor, *A Sourcebook About Liturgy* (Chicago: Liturgy Training Publications, 1994). A gathering together of beloved texts about liturgy.

Lawrence J. Johnson, *A Singer's Companion to the Church Year* (Beltsville MD: Pastoral Press, 1995). A guide to each Sunday's liturgy in years A, B and C with informative and inspirational commentary.

Aidan Kavanagh, *Elements of Rite* (Collegeville MN: The Liturgical Press, 1982). "A Handbook of Liturgical Style," with great insight into ritual and ministry.

Linda Osborn, *Good Liturgy, Small Parishes* (Chicago: Liturgy Training Publications, 1994). A modest book for celebrations in places of modest means.

Gerard A. Pottebaum, *The Rites of People* (Beltsville MD: Pastoral Press, 1992). An exploration of ritual-making that helps connect Sunday liturgy with the entire human experience.

The Cantor in
Liturgical Celebration

The cantor needs to prepare for liturgy in several ways. First, of course, you need to have learned the music and rehearsed it with the instrumentalists, preferably in the worship space, before arriving at church. There is no time to learn music or to rehearse adequately immediately before a liturgy. There is other preparation that must be made on the day of the liturgy.

Preparation

Allow at least fifteen minutes for vocal warm-up (vocalization). You can do this at home, in your car or, if space is available, at church. Begin with gentle vocalization, such as humming. Then vocalize using your most beautiful vowel sounds in the best part of your range (the best sounding and most easily produced notes in your voice). If you have time, sing through all of the material you will be using in the day's liturgy. At the very least, sing through any spots that were difficult in rehearsal. Read through the texts so that their content is uppermost in your mind.

Your attire will depend primarily upon the expectations of the assembly. What you wear should not distract from what you are about. Keep in mind that it is your task to serve God by serving the assembly. If your attire sets you apart from the assembly because you are overdressed or underdressed, or if your clothing calls attention to itself, you may find it more difficult to perform your ministry.

Arrive at least fifteen minutes before the liturgy is to begin. If you are going to introduce new material to the assembly, to review material or simply to warm up their voices, you should arrive earlier. Check in with the presider and any other musicians involved. You should confirm such things as the content and length of introductions and musical interludes, as well as the number of verses or stanzas to be sung. Review what parts the presider is to sing or intone. Clarify any questions regarding the day's liturgy. It might be necessary to check in with the lector if you are using the ambo for the psalm, or to agree on a period of silence between the readings.

Be aware that presiders and others are also trying to prepare; allow them to do so. This is not a good time to make changes or offer suggestions, to try something spontaneously, or to conduct any business that could better be handled at another place and time.

You should discreetly set up your music and check your microphone at least ten minutes before you are to begin. This preparation should take place before the people have begun to assemble. If ministers are running around and making last-minute adjustments right up to the beginning of worship, there is an atmosphere of a performance, which is not respectful of the assembly. Carefully timed preparation will make you feel good about what you are doing, and that feeling will be communicated to the assembly.

Once all your preparations are made in good time, you can relax and greet a few people in the assembly, then quiet yourself for the liturgy. These quiet moments can block out any distractions and allow you to enter fully into the liturgy, even as you perform this public ministry.

The place from which you sing is important. It is essential for you to be seen by the assembly. At the same time, it is important for you to be within working distance of any instrumentalists with whom you will be singing. It is difficult to accommodate both these needs if the organ (console or pipes) is in a rear gallery. In that case, you can work from the front with unaccompanied repertoire, or you can be accompanied by other instruments situated near you. A cantor should rarely if ever be a solo voice emanating from the choir loft.

Teaching Music to the Assembly

You will occasionally need to introduce new material to the assembly before the liturgy begins. Specific details of how this should be done, and how frequently, should be decided by those in charge of music in consultation with others involved in the liturgy.

How to Prepare on Liturgy Days

- Dress appropriately
- Vocalize
- Arrive early
- Check in with other musicians and with the presider
- Set up music and check the microphone
- Briefly greet others
- Quiet yourself

You should write out and perhaps commit to memory what you are going to say to introduce this music to the assembly. Speaking without a prepared text usually leads to rambling. Be concise. And always have your text in front of you — just in case.

Speak clearly and distinctly. If you are nervous, you will probably speak too quickly or too quietly. Fight these inclinations. Believe that what you have to say is important and convey that feeling to the assembly. Speak deliberately.

Your ability to use a microphone well is important. Practice beforehand, without the assembly present, to find the right distance from which to speak and to sing. Generally, this is between six and twelve inches from the microphone, but will vary according to the type of microphone, the volume at which the microphone is set and the acoustics of the church. If you find that the microphone does not pick up your voice well enough from six inches away, do not move in closer to increase the volume. This can jumble diction, compounding the problem. Instead, use your ability to project. Keep in mind that you are not speaking intimately to a single individual, but addressing a group of people.

When you are preparing to introduce or review music for the assembly before a liturgy, the piece itself and your method of introduction will help you determine what to say. For a short refrain it may be enough to have the instrumentalist(s) play the refrain, to sing it yourself, and then to have the assembly sing it. You might say something like this:

"Good morning. (pause) Today and in the coming weeks we will be singing a refrain that may be new to some of you. It can be found in . . . on page . . . . Please follow along as I sing through it and then repeat after me."

After the assembly sings with you, you might continue with a statement of how or when the refrain will be used. Conclude with a simple "thank you."

Reflection in Preparation

Sit down in your place. Close or lower your eyes and breathe deeply. Breathe slowly and rhythmically. Block out any distractions and focus on how you feel, physically and emotionally. If there are any unpleasant feelings — tiredness, nervousness, concerns — let go of them by focusing on your breathing.

Next, focus on something uplifting. This might be a psalm or song from the day's liturgy or a reflection on the love of God. If it helps you to think of a specific prayer, savor each word and phrase. Otherwise, simply pray in whatever way is yours. Reflect on why you are there and what it means to serve.

Come back to the present by becoming aware of the assembly. Look around you. Know that these people, yourself included, are the body of Christ, the church, met here to give thanks and praise and to be fed by God's word and the holy communion.

A good resource for this time of prayer is the book *Prayers of Those Who Make Music* (Chicago: Liturgy Training Publications, 1984). It can easily be tucked into a purse or pocket, making it readily available for personal reflection or shared prayer.

If the piece is longer or more complex, you might begin by reading the text aloud while the assembly follows along, or by inviting them to read aloud with you. This is also a good way to highlight the text and to get people involved in its content. Don't teach the assembly a lengthy hymn by reading every stanza — but do read a few. If you love the words and handle them well, your delight will be catching.

How would you read this text?

Love divine, all loves excelling,
Joy of heav'n, to earth come down!
Fix in us thy humble dwelling,
All thy faithful mercies crown.
Jesus, thou art all compassion,
Pure unbounded love thou art;
Visit us with thy salvation,
Enter ev'ry trembling heart.

Come, almighty to deliver,
Let us all thy life receive;
Suddenly return and never,
Never more thy temples leave.
Thee we would be always blessing,
Serve thee as thy hosts above,
Pray, and praise thee without ceasing,
Glory in thy precious love.

Finish then thy new creation,
Pure and spotless let us be;
Let us see thy great salvation
Perfectly restored in thee!
Changed from glory into glory,
Till in heav'n we take our place,
Till we cast our crowns before thee,
Lost in wonder, love and praise.

This text by Charles Wesley comes from his 1747 collection, *Redemption Hymns.* Reading hymns together this way can help people to embrace texts and to think of hymns in their entirety.

A wonderful way to teach hymns or longer refrains is a method known as "lining out." A piece is executed continuously, one phrase at a time. Each phrase is sung by the cantor and repeated immediately by the assembly. In the following example the cantor sings the hymn four measures at a time, with the people immediately repeating each phrase.

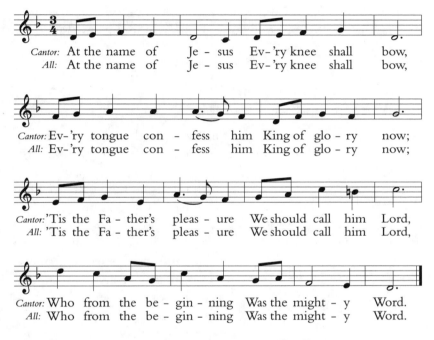

Cantor: At the name of Je - sus Ev-'ry knee shall bow,
All: At the name of Je - sus Ev-'ry knee shall bow,

Cantor: Ev-'ry tongue con - fess him King of glo - ry now;
All: Ev-'ry tongue con - fess him King of glo - ry now;

Cantor: 'Tis the Fa - ther's pleas - ure We should call him Lord,
All: 'Tis the Fa - ther's pleas - ure We should call him Lord,

Cantor: Who from the be - gin - ning Was the might - y Word.
All: Who from the be - gin - ning Was the might - y Word.

The stanza may then be sung in its entirety by all.

There are many ways to introduce or review music with the assembly. What is essential is that the language is clear and hospitable, that the introduction is carefully executed and that you, the cantor, believe in what you are doing and asking the assembly to do. Make every effort not to condescend ("After I sing for you, please try to repeat the refrain!"), to entertain ("You'll really love this one!") or to chastise ("You're not singing!").

You should hope for a wholehearted response, but do not be disappointed if the response is less than enthusiastic. Some people are slow to respond and others may never participate, for a variety of reasons. People should not be judged harshly for it, nor should you blame yourself. Be consistent and take the long view.

Sound liturgical practice suggests that once a parish has found and learned music of quality, it should be used through a season or over a number of weeks of Ordinary Time. Those pieces that are used only in Lent, for example, might be used throughout Lent, and year after year. A piece used only once a year (at the washing of feet, for example) should be used each year. This continuity, when the music is worthy, shows respect for the assembly and the liturgy. Often, music ministers tire of a piece long before the assembly. This is because music ministers have much greater exposure to the music through continued practice and multiplication of liturgical celebrations. Try to approach familiar music in fresh, new ways each time it is used.

Physical Communication and Animation of the Assembly

Gestures are an important part of inviting people to sing. Let your arms rest comfortably at your sides as you sing. When it is time for the assembly to sing, breathe with them and raise your arms, with palms turned upward, to about shoulder height. The position should resemble one you would use to embrace someone. Let your arms remain in this position for a few seconds, and then let them fall slowly to their original position at your sides. If you hold your music in your hand, you will be limited to one arm for your gestures. Do only what is necessary to get response and no more. Repetitive superflous gestures will be tuned out, and the cantor ignored. Understand that your gesture can and will make something happen. Practice hailing a cab or calling children to hurry along. Relating your gestures to other experiences can make them more effective.

Another visual cue, the raising of the eyes to take in the assembly, should accompany any gesture. In some cases, raising

---

Speaking to the Assembly

Your tone should be cordial and persuasive. Imagine that you are greeting friends whom you care for deeply. Isn't this really the case?

For practice, write a thank-you note to someone. Read it aloud. Use that same warmth when addressing the assembly.

When you use a microphone, speak and sing as if it were not there. Your voice will have more energy and intensity.

Be careful not to pop "b" or "p" when speaking and singing into the microphone. This will probably not happen if you are far enough away from the microphone.

Observing Others

Make a point of observing other cantors, lectors and presiders. Take note of both positive and negative aspects of their body language. Are there superfluous motions and gestures? Are deliberate gestures big enough to be seen? Are they too big? Does the person appear confident? Why, or why not? What effect does eye contact from the person have on you? Does the minister have any special affectation?

the eyes or nodding the head is a sufficient indication for people to sing. Some assemblies will sing enthusiastically with no physical cue at all, but every cantor should be comfortable with gestures. The use of gestures will then be determined by the needs of the assembly and not by the limitations of the cantor.

It will not always be possible for the cantor to breathe with the assembly. Sometimes there is an overlap between the cantor's part and the people's response. In such a case the gesture must still precede the entrance of the assembly as described earlier, but without the actual intake of air by the cantor.

Body language in general should be attended to very carefully. You need to appear confident, but not cocky. If you fidget or avoid people's eyes, you will make the assembly uncomfortable. If you come on too strong, the members of the assembly might react by withdrawing. You should not be overly casual in your demeanor, nor should you be stiff or affected. It also helps to smile, if you can be natural doing so.

Move into your position deliberately and without haste. Do not move before you need to move. Your chair should be close enough to your music stand and microphone that you do not have to walk far. Remember that your movement sets an atmosphere for worship. It should have a certain dignity. When you have finished singing something, wait for the conclusion of the instrumental part and another moment before sitting down. You do not want to give the impression that you are eager for this to be over. If you seem impatient, others will become impatient.

Like all members of the assembly, your attention should always be on what is happening in the liturgy. The liturgy is yours to do as a full, active and conscious participant — and exemplary member of the assembly. Try not to daydream, fuss with your music, hum, audibly clear your throat or jingle change in your pocket.

When you are singing before the assembly, be careful not to make unnecessary movements, especially unconscious or habitual movements in time with the music. This will distract the assembly from what you are trying to express. Do not shift your weight from one foot to the other, rock back and forth, rise up on your toes or squat on bent knees. Never use your hands to check for a tense throat, neck or jaw. Never cup your ear in order to hear yourself better. Do not conduct in time to the music or strike affected poses, such as hands clasped before you. Such movements are usually done unconsciously, so you may need to rely on the observations of others. Practice in front of a mirror to eliminate idiosyncrasies like these.

Some kinds of movement are absolutely suited to musical performance. An inhibited and rigid appearance can be as distracting as any mentioned earlier.

It is proper to sing with the assembly as a way of encouraging their singing and as a way of fulfilling your own role as a member of the assembly, but your voice should never overpower the singing of the assembly. Too often the cantor ends up singing in place of

Making Gestures

Choose one of the refrains below with which to practice your gestures. If possible, practice in front of a mirror. Sing through the refrain as if you were intoning it for the assembly. Inhale and raise your arms (and your eyes, if you have been looking only at the music) as if cuing the singing of the assembly. Sing the refrain again and cue the imaginary assembly without using arms and hands. Try again using only one hand. Do this with refrains that begin on a variety of beats and fractions of beats, being certain that the gesture immediately precedes the singing of the assembly.

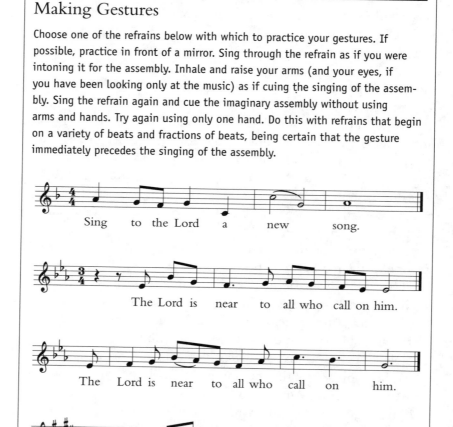

the assembly. If your own singing is amplified over the singing of the assembly, some may feel inclined to just listen. Others may feel defeated and decide that their singing is unimportant. If you are singing at a microphone, step back or step aside when it is the assembly's turn to sing. It is easy to be seduced by the sound of your own voice. Strive to hear and to love the assembly's voice. Know with certainty that — given worthy music — an assembly will sing better if they are not hearing your amplified voice.

An exception to this rule against leading with the sound of the cantor's amplified voice would be when the singing is not accompanied by instruments. Even then, the cantor's leadership should be gentle enough so that the assembly has to listen carefully, and so that the leader can listen to the assembly.

If an organ is used, it should be the organ that leads and sustains the singing of the assembly. If other instruments are used, they should be capable of leading the assembly.

Dealing with the Unexpected

Unexpected situations can arise in the course of a liturgy. Everything should be done to prevent such situations, of course, but when they occur they should be handled calmly, with common sense and always with mutual charity.

When a microphone seems to fail, do not fidget with the microphone or its cord. If there is an on-off switch, check to see that it is on. Do not tap the mike or blow into it. If your singing is well focused, it will project without electronic amplification. Don't let the assembly know that there is a problem.

If you make a mistake, do not panic. Everyone makes mistakes. Do what needs to be done and go on. Do not draw attention to your mistakes by getting angry, upset or silly. These are things that might come through in your body language if you are not in control. Similarly, do not show anger or dismay because of malfunctioning objects, crying babies or unresponsive people.

Cantor and Assembly

Ask yourself the following hard questions:

- When the singing of the assembly is strong, do I get louder in order to be heard above it?
- Am I so certain that the assembly will not sing that I sing their parts for them — right into the microphone?
- Do I attempt to control the tempo of congregational singing, hoping the organist will follow?
- Do I enjoy the singing of the assembly, or am I impatient until it is my turn to sing alone?

Evaluation

After the liturgy, make note of anything that might have gone wrong between you and the other liturgical ministers. Ask the following questions:

- Was there adequate preparation?
- Rehearsal?
- Communication?
- Cooperation?
- What might be done to avoid mistakes in the future?

Do not confront other ministers immediately after the liturgy. Find some time during the week to sit down and calmly discuss your concerns. Liturgical ministers are as human and fragile as anyone else. The last thing anyone needs is an "instant analysis" of their performance.

Never act judgmentally toward other ministers or members of the assembly. If the presider forgets that the Gloria is to be sung — even if the presider deliberately decides it should be recited — do not publicly show that anything is wrong. If a lector begins to recite a psalm when you have spent hours preparing that psalm, let it go. Such matters can be calmly addressed after the liturgy. Never reprimand or chide the assembly for their apparent lack of involvement or for poor singing. Uncharitable behavior can only undermine what a cantor is about. Furthermore, people will be more likely to show charity toward you if you act in kind.

FURTHER READING: LITURGICAL MINISTRY

These resources, although not specifically about the ministry of the cantor, will be helpful to you in proclaiming the word and in leading prayer.

Joseph M. Champlin, *An Important Office of Immense Love* (Ramsey NJ: Paulist Press, 1980).

James Dallen, *The Dilemma of Priestless Sundays* (Chicago: Liturgy Training Publications, 1994).

Kathleen Hughes, RCSJ, *Lay Presiding: The Art of Leading Prayer* (Collegeville MN: The Liturgical Press, 1981).

Aelred R. Rosser, *A Well-Trained Tongue: Formation in the Ministry of the Reader* (Chicago: Liturgy Training Publications, 1996).

Workbook for Lectors and Gospel Readers (Chicago: Liturgy Training Publications, annual).

The Cantor's Songs

The psalms constitute the largest and most significant body of material for which the cantor is responsible. They are integral to celebrating the eucharist, the Liturgy of the Hours and most of the church's other rites. The psalms are essential to the structure of these rites and to our feasts and seasons.

The church's psalter includes the 150 psalms from the biblical Book of Psalms. Our psalter also includes other poems, usually referred to as canticles, from both the Hebrew Scriptures and the New Testament. The New Testament itself tells us that Jesus and his followers prayed and cherished the psalms. The church continues to pray and sing psalms and canticles, finding in them a large and beautiful repertoire. The psalms have taught us how to speak before God, alone and as a church. The psalms embrace all the passions and moods and conditions of humankind. When we sing the psalms, our voices join with Jews and Christians of our day and of generations past. It is important to remember that the psalms and Hebrew canticles belonged first to the Jewish people, and to try to understand them in their Jewish context.

In Roman Catholic liturgy, the song between the first and second scripture readings is to be drawn from the psalter. The lectionary, the book that contains the order of scripture readings to be used in liturgy throughout the year, designates a psalm for every day and season of the liturgical year. The lectionary also provides alternative psalms that may be used between the first and second scripture readings. These alternatives, which may be used on all the Sundays of a given season, are the seasonal psalms. They can be found at #175 in the lectionary, and the seasonal responses, at #174. (These numbers may vary when the revised lectionary is published in the late 1990s.) The National Conference of Catholic Bishops, the NCCB, allows any translation of these psalms to be used after the first reading, even metrical psalmody, as long as the psalm is sung. Some texts often suggested for the psalm between the readings are "based on" a psalm, but these should be avoided.

Consider the seasonal psalms. Each of them — Psalm 96 at Christmastime or Psalm 51 during Lent, for example — constitutes a sort of theme song for its season, a source of meditation on the season that returns fresh and new each year. The seasonal psalms are particularly useful because of their ability to set a season apart. The repetition of one psalm over several weeks allows the assembly to learn its refrain by heart; only then are people truly able to make the psalm their own, to ponder its poetry and images and to experience this form of prayer. This way of praying is not simply one option among many but is the very model of all Jewish and Christian prayer.

Various Ways of Singing the Psalms

RESPONSORIAL   The most common way of singing the psalms is the responsorial form. This form is designated for the psalm between the readings at Mass. It is also used in celebrating the Liturgy of the Hours and other rites, such as penance services and the anointing of the sick. The name does not refer to making a "response" to a reading, but only to the form of rendition used.

In the responsorial form the cantor or choir intones the refrain (often called the antiphon), and the assembly repeats it. The cantor or choir then sings the first stanza, usually containing several verses of the psalm, and the assembly then repeats the refrain. The cantor or choir and assembly alternate stanza and refrain until the psalm concludes with a final singing of the refrain.

The following are examples of the responsorial form. The first, Psalm 134, is a traditional night psalm. The canticle of Mary, also known as the Magnificat, has long been a part of evening prayer. The canticle of Zechariah, the Benedictus, is part of morning prayer. Both canticles are from the Gospel according to Luke.

Refrain

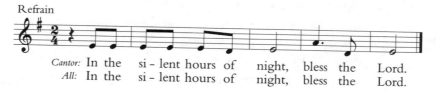

1. O come, bless the Lord, all you who serve the Lord, who stand in the house of the Lord, in the courts of the house of our God.

All: In the si - lent hours of night, bless the Lord.

2. Lift up your hands to the ho - ly place and bless the Lord through the night.

All: In the si - lent hours of night, bless the Lord.

3. May the Lord bless you from Zi - on, he who made both heav - en and earth.

All: In the si - lent hours of night, bless the Lord.

Antiphon for Canticle of Mary

I ac-claim the great-ness of the Lord. I de-

light in God my sav-ior.

Antiphon for Canticle of Zechariah

Lord, guide our feet on the way to peace.

Tone for Canticles of Mary and Zechariah

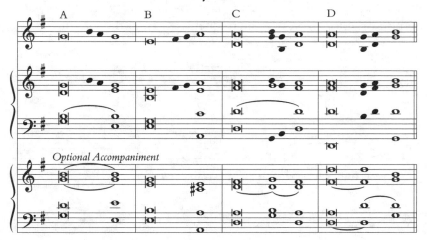

Canticle of Mary

I acclaim the greatness of the Lord,
I delight in God my savior,
who regarded my humble state.
Truly from this day on
all ages will call me blest.

For God, wonderful in power,
has used that strength for me.
Holy the name of the Lord!
whose mercy embraces the faithful,
one generation to the next.

The mighty arm of God
scatters the proud in their conceit,
pulls tyrants from their thrones,
and raises up the humble.
The Lord fills the starving
and lets the rich go hungry.

God rescues lowly Israel,
recalling the promise of mercy,
the promise made to our ancestors,
to Abraham's heirs for ever.

Canticle of Zechariah

Praise the Lord, the God of Israel,
who shepherds the people
    and sets them free.

God raises from David's house
a child with power to save.
Through the holy prophets
God promised in ages past
to save us from enemy hands,
from the grip of all who hate us.

The Lord favored our ancestors
recalling the sacred covenant,
the pledge to our ancestor Abraham,
to free us from our enemies,

so we might worship without fear
and be holy and just all our days.

And you, child, will be called
Prophet of the Most High,
for you will come to prepare
a pathway for the Lord
by teaching the people salvation
through forgiveness of their sin.

Out of God's deepest mercy
a dawn will come from on high,
light for those shadowed by death,
a guide for our feet on the
    way to peace.

This excerpt from the Canticle of the Lamb demonstrates a litany-like method of rendering a psalm. This is a variation of the responsorial form. Notice the frequent return of the refrain.

Sometimes the initial intonation of the refrain by the cantor is omitted either because it is already known or for the sake of time. This unnecessary elimination often confuses the assembly, thus taking the liturgy away from them. Likewise, it is a mistake for the cantor to intone only the first half of a refrain, unless it is composed of two identical phrases.

In the responsorial method, the cantor's verses are sometimes set to a formula known as a "psalm tone." This is a simple melodic pattern in which a number of words are sung to a single pitch.

The psalm verses may be "pointed" or otherwise marked to correspond to the specific tone. The traditional Gregorian psalm tones have been supplemented by many newly composed tones, such as those found in the *ICEL Lectionary Music* collection, *The People's Mass Book* choral edition (World Library Publications), *Respond and Acclaim* (Oregon Catholic Press), *Worship* (GIA Publications), the settings by Michel Guimont in *Gather, Second Edition* and *Gather Comprehensive* (GIA Publications), and most recently, *Psalms for Morning and Evening Prayer* (Liturgy Training Publications).

The following canticle is an example of a pointed text and its corresponding tone.

Refrain

Je - sus is the im-age of the un - seen God: the first - born of all cre - a - tion.

Omit for 3-line stanza

1. Let us give thanks to the Fàther
   for having made you wórthy
   to share the lot of the sáints in light.

2. He rescued us from the power of dàrkness
   and brought us into the kingdom of his beloved Són.
   Through him we hàve redemption,
   the forgiveness óf our sins.

3. He is the image of the invisible Gòd,
   the first-born of all créatures.
   In him everything in heaven and on earth wàs created,
   things visible ánd invisible.

4. All were created through hìm;
   all were created for hím.
   He is before all èlse that is.
   In him everything contínues in being.

5. It is he who is head of the body, the chùrch;
   he who is the begínning,

the first-born òf the dead,
    so that primacy may be hís in everything.

    Here is another method of marking a text for its corresponding tone. The *intonation* is a kind of introduction that occurs only at the beginning of a stanza. The *tenor* is the note to which a large portion of the psalm is chanted. The *mediant* accommodates a stanza with an odd number of phrases, and provides melodic interest. The mediant is usually denoted by an accent, but here it is denoted by bold type, as is the final *cadence*.

Refrain

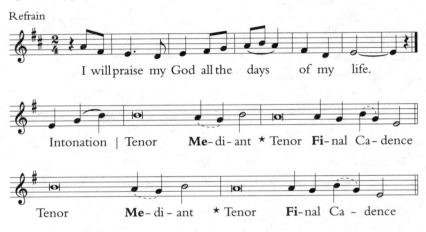

I will praise my God all the days of my life.

Intonation | Tenor   **Me**- di- ant ★ Tenor **Fi**- nal Ca - dence

Tenor   **Me**- di - ant ★ Tenor **Fi**- nal Ca - dence

O God, | you are my God whom I seek;'
    for you my flesh pines and my **soul** thirsts ★
    like the earth, parched, lifeless and **with**out water. *R.*

Thus have | I gazed toward you in the **sanc**tuary ★
    to see your power **and** your glory,
For your kindness is a greater **good** than life; ★
    my lips shall **glo**rify you. *R.*

Thus will | I bless you **while** I live; ★
    lifting up my hands, I will **call** upon your name.
As with the riches of a banquet shall my soul be **sat**isfied, ★
    and with exultant lips my **mouth** shall praise you. *R.*

    Sometimes the psalm tone is written out with the text, as in this excerpt.

Refrain

As morn-ing breaks I look to you, O God, to

be my strength this day, al - le - lu - ia.

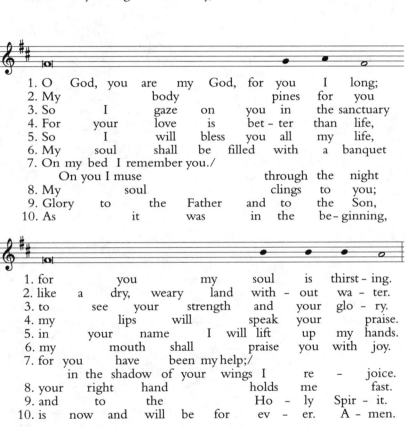

1. O God, you are my God, for you I long;
2. My body pines for you
3. So I gaze on you in the sanctuary
4. For your love is bet - ter than life,
5. So I will bless you all my life,
6. My soul shall be filled with a banquet
7. On my bed I remember you./
   On you I muse through the night
8. My soul clings to you;
9. Glory to the Father and to the Son,
10. As it was in the be - ginning,

1. for you my soul is thirst - ing.
2. like a dry, weary land with - out wa - ter.
3. to see your strength and your glo - ry.
4. my lips will speak your praise.
5. in your name I will lift up my hands.
6. my mouth shall praise you with joy.
7. for you have been my help;/
   in the shadow of your wings I re - joice.
8. your right hand holds me fast.
9. and to the Ho - ly Spir - it.
10. is now and will be for ev - er. A - men.

Gelineau psalm tones, named for the French composer Joseph
Gelineau, exemplify another formula. They are based on a type
of rhythmic organization called "sprung rhythm." Each line of a
verse has a certain number of stressed syllables. Each stressed syllable corresponds to the stressed beat in each measure. The syllables
falling upon the long note can be sung in a number of ways,
reflecting the rhythm and stresses of speech. There may be unstressed
introductory syllables before the first stressed syllable, and so an
introductory pulse is needed after the refrain and before each verse

begins. The *Gelineau Gradual* offers complete instructions for interpreting its psalms.

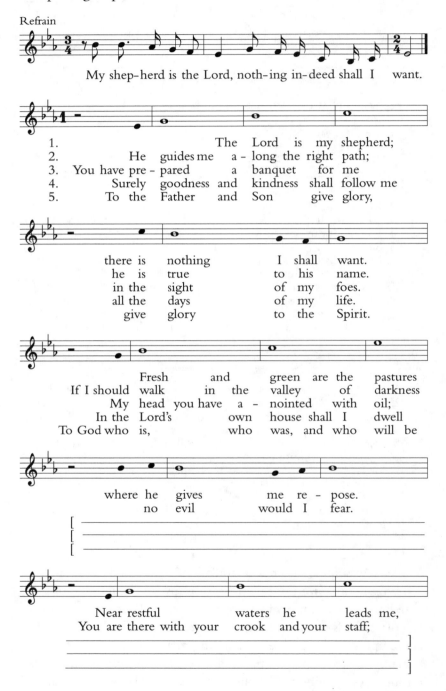

Refrain

My shep-herd is the Lord, noth-ing in-deed shall I want.

1.   The Lord is my shepherd;
2.   He guides me a - long the right path;
3. You have pre - pared   a banquet for me
4.   Surely goodness and kindness shall follow me
5.   To the Father and Son   give glory,

there is   nothing   I shall   want.
he is   true   to his   name.
in the   sight   of my   foes.
all the   days   of my   life.
give   glory   to the   Spirit.

Fresh   and   green are the   pastures
If I should walk   in the   valley   of   darkness
My head you have a - nointed with   oil;
In the Lord's   own   house shall I   dwell
To God who is,   who   was, and who will be

where he   gives   me re - pose.
no   evil   would I   fear.

[
[
[

Near restful   waters he   leads me,
You are there with your crook and your staff;

]
]
]

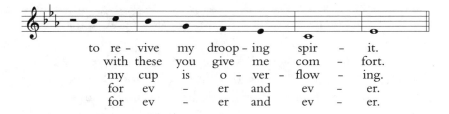

to	re –	vive	my	droop –	ing	spir	–	it.
	with	these	you	give	me	com	–	fort.
	my	cup	is	o –	ver –	flow	–	ing.
	for	ev	–	er	and	ev	–	er.
	for	ev	–	er	and	ev	–	er.

THROUGH-COMPOSED   The term "through-composed" is often misunderstood. It refers to psalm settings rendered by cantor or choir alone. This method is commonly combined with the responsorial form. The intention of the composer is to find music that conveys the emotional content and literary structure of a specific text. The result usually involves little repetition of musical material. Through-composed settings are often the most enjoyable for the cantor, but that should not be the most important factor is selecting psalm settings for liturgical use.

CANTILLATION   Cantillation is a kind of half-speech, half-song which is improvised by the cantor to a specific psalm text. This method predates Christianity. There are traditional guidelines for this improvisation, such as the mode or key of a piece, and certain standard formulas for pitch selection. Clearly, such "improvisation" is not intended to be entirely spontaneous. This method should only be attempted by advanced cantors, and only after careful preparation. The more limited your pitch selection (perhaps four or five pitches), the easier it will be. A good place to begin might be the prayers of intercession.

MIXED   A combination of various methods is referred to as "mixed media." An example might be a recitation of the psalm text to an instrumental accompaniment, with a sung refrain.

ANTIPHONAL   The antiphonal method of psalmody requires that the assembly be divided into two groups, one of which may be the choir. The groups take turns singing equal portions of the psalm, usually to the same melody. This melody is often a formula or psalm tone as described above. A refrain may be sung by both groups together at the beginning and end of the psalm.

METRICAL   Sometimes psalms are given metrical settings. The psalm is organized into stanzas, with each stanza sung to the same notes and rhythms, like the verses of a hymn. In fact, this method is often called the "hymn model." To fit the requirements of the meter, the text of the psalm is usually paraphrased, although this may obscure the original content. The entire psalm is sung by everyone. A good example is the hymn "All people that on earth do dwell," which is a paraphrase of Psalm 100. Liturgical law no longer prohibits the use of metrical psalmody between the readings in the liturgy of the word at eucharist, but metrical settings are seldom among the translations designated for liturgical use. Still, metrical psalms are wonderfully suited to accompany the various processions in the liturgy.

The term "metrical" is sometimes used for any psalm given a rhythmic notation, but this is not an accurate use of the term.

Other Cantor Repertoire

The cantor may also be responsible for solo passages within songs and hymns. These pieces often give the assembly a recurring refrain to sing, with intervening sung statements or verses by the cantor. Thus they resemble the responsorial psalmody already discussed and the litanies described below. In some cases, the assembly sings a continual refrain with the cantor singing the verses simultaneously in an "overlay" fashion. This is called an ostinato refrain.

LITANIES A litany is a sung prayer that often has a set refrain to be sung by the assembly in alternation with invocations sung by the cantor. It may accompany a ritual action, such as the breaking of the bread ("Lamb of God") or the procession to the font (Litany of the Saints). The church has many litany prayers. Cantors should become familiar with those discussed here.

In the litany of the penitential rite, the presider, deacon or cantor may call upon Jesus as "Lord" or "Christ," followed by a short statement ("Lord, you bring glad tidings to the poor"). The presider, deacon or cantor concludes the statement with "Lord (Christ), have mercy." The people respond, echoing the conclusion.

The "Lamb of God" litany accompanies the breaking of the bread. The sacramentary says that the litany is to continue all through the breaking of the bread. The cantor may call upon Christ by various descriptive names, always beginning and ending with "Lamb of God." Other titles might include "Bread of life," "Prince of peace," and other scriptural images of Christ. The people respond each time with "Have mercy on us" and conclude with "Grant us peace."

The general intercessions or prayer of the faithful is a litany in which the deacon or cantor intones petitions for the church, the world, the oppressed and the local community. The people may respond to each intention by singing "Lord, have mercy" or "Lord, hear our prayer." The urgency of these prayers may be intensified by overlapping the leader's prayer or intention and the assembly's response.

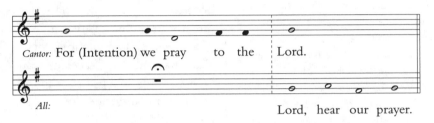

Cantor: For (Intention) we pray to the Lord.

All: Lord, hear our prayer.

In the Litany of the Saints the cantor names or invokes the saints. The people traditionally respond to each invocation by chanting: "Pray for us," though not in every contemporary setting. (We do not pray to the saints, but ask them to intercede on our behalf.) In the traditional litany it is important that the flow of invocation and response be continuous; a litany does its work by catching everyone in its rhythm so that we are freed for complete immersion in the sound of prayer. Other litanies of this type include the Litany of the Holy Name, the Litany of Saint Joseph, and the Litany of Loretto, which is also known as the Litany of the Blessed Virgin.

GOSPEL ACCLAMATIONS Gospel acclamations are another important part of cantor repertoire. Outside of the Lenten season, the alleluia is sung before the proclamation of the gospel. During Lent, one of the following acclamations is sung, or the acclamation is omitted.

Praise and honor to you, Lord Jesus Christ.
Glory and praise to you, Lord Jesus Christ.
Glory to you, Word of God, Lord Jesus Christ.
Praise to you, Lord Jesus Christ, King of endless glory.

Acclamations

The acclamations of the eucharistic prayer belong first and foremost to the assembly. Rare occasions may call for music that requires a cantor for these acclamations (for example, a one-time gathering of people who have no common repertoire). A call and response setting for the eucharistic acclamations is only a teaching tool, and should not be used once the assembly knows the acclamations thoroughly.

The appropriate verse to accompany the gospel acclamation on a specific day can be found in the lectionary. This verse is sung by the cantor. The accompaniment editions of most Roman Catholic hymnals and missalettes offer settings of the gospel acclamations and corresponding tones for the recitation of the cantor's verse. The gospel acclamation with its verse is intended to accompany the gospel procession; both music and procession lead directly to the proclamation of the gospel. The sacramentary is clear that the gospel acclamation is to be sung; when for some reason this cannot be done, it is to be omitted.

GLORIA   The Gloria may also be a part of cantor repertoire if sung alternately with the assembly. Many settings have been composed to make the musical rendition of this difficult and lengthy text more accessible, but some would argue that such settings go against the natural form of the text. If the cantor has no special part, but doubles the choir or the assembly, the cantor's voice should not be amplified. The cantor may visually animate the assembly in this song of praise.

PROCLAMATIONS   The cantor should also be familiar with the various proclamations that are designated for certain times in the church year. The Christmas and Epiphany proclamations can be found in the annual *Sourcebook for Sundays and Seasons* (Liturgy Training Publications), and the Easter proclamation, Exsultet, can be found in the sacramentary. The Exsultet, the only proclamation designated as part of the liturgy, is sung at the Easter Vigil. See the chapter, "Exsultet," which begins on page 77.

Musical, Liturgical and Pastoral Judgments

In selecting music for liturgical celebration, three judgments should be kept in mind. These are the musical judgment, the liturgical judgment and the pastoral judgment.

The cantor is not often the person who selects the music, but should understand why certain pieces are used. The informed cantor can better serve the assembly.

The importance and application of these three judgments are explained in *Music in Catholic Worship.* This brief document and *Liturgical Music Today* were prepared by the Bishops' Committee on the Liturgy as guidelines and directives for the church in the United States. Every cantor should read and reread these documents, which are available in *The Liturgy Documents: A Parish Resource,* published by Liturgy Training Publications. This crucial matter is further developed in *The Milwaukee Symposia for Church Composers,* also published by Liturgy Training Publications.

Seasonal Psalms

The seasonal psalms can serve as a unifying element throughout
a liturgical season. The complete list of psalms for each Sunday,
feast and season throughout the church year can be found in the
lectionary. *Sourcebook for Sundays and Seasons,* published annually
by Liturgy Training Publications, suggests many specific settings for
seasonal psalmody.

ADVENT
Psalm 25

CHRISTMAS
Psalm 98

LENT
Psalm 51
Psalm 98
Psalm 130

HOLY WEEK
Psalm 22

EASTER VIGIL
Psalm 136

EASTERTIME
Psalm 118

ORDINARY TIME
Psalm 19
Psalm 27
Psalm 34
Psalm 63
Psalm 95
Psalm 100
Psalm 103
Psalm 145

LAST WEEKS OF ORDINARY TIME
Psalm 122

SINGING AND PRAYING THE PSALMS

Many fine collections of responsorial psalms are available. Among them are:

ICEL Lectionary Music (Chicago: GIA Publications, Inc., 1982). Settings of some of the seasonal psalms and responses.

Joseph Gelineau, *The Gelineau Gradual* (Chicago: GIA Publications, Inc., 1977). Settings of the portions of the psalter used for Sundays and principal feasts.

Praise God in Song (Chicago: GIA Publications, Inc., 1979). A good resource for psalmody within the Liturgy of the Hours.

Psalms for the Cantor (Schiller Park IL: World Library Publications, 1986). Settings of the portions of the psalter used for Sundays and feasts, as well as seasonal psalms, in seven volumes organized by liturgical season.

Respond and Acclaim (Portland OR: OCP Publications, 1987). Psalm refrains with corresponding tones for Sundays and feasts.

The following translations of the psalms strive for inclusive language. They have not been approved for liturgical use, but according to present norms could be used, if sung, for the responsorial psalm at Mass.

The Grail Psalter (Chicago: GIA Publications, Inc., 1994).

ICEL, *The Psalter* (Chicago: Liturgy Training Publications, 1995). Psalm tones for this translation were composed by Howard Hughes. They also appear in *Morning and Evening Prayer* (Chicago: Liturgy Training Publications, 1995).

There are many useful resources for understanding and praying psalm texts. Here are a few.

Walter Brueggemann, *The Message of the Psalms: A Theological Commentary* (Minneapolis: Augsburg, 1984).

Walter Brueggemann, *Praying the Psalms* (Winona: Saint Mary's Press, 1982).

George A. F. Knight, *Psalms,* Volumes 1 and 2 (Philadelphia: The Westminster Press, 1982).

Leopold Sabourin, *The Psalms: Their Origin and Meaning* (New York: Alba House, 1974).

Massey Shepherd, *The Psalms in Christian Worship* (Minneapolis: Augsburg, 1976).

Carroll Stuhlmueller, *Psalms I & II, Old Testament Message: A Biblical-Theological Commentary,* Volume 21 (Wilmington: Michael Glazier, 1983).

The Cantor as a Singer

Beginning and advanced cantors alike should have a fundamental knowledge of their vocal instrument, and they
should apply that knowledge to their singing. This will make it much
easier to pinpoint and resolve vocal problems; it may even prevent
serious problems.

A cantor must be willing to abandon personal inhibitions in the
pursuit of vocal skill. It is said that one's reach should exceed one's
grasp, or what's a heaven for? Vocal study does not mean cultivating
an "operatic" voice. Folk singers, pop singers, singers of art songs —
as well as those who sing opera — all require training and practice
in order to develop the beauty, control and consistency that will allow
them to communicate in their chosen idiom.

Of course, any highly stylized approach is to be avoided by the
cantor. Sometimes performers go out of their way to develop a
style that sets them apart or makes a statement. A cantor with such
an approach will diminish the power of the texts and may even
prevent the participation of certain members of the assembly. If
technique and musicianship allow it, cantors should be versatile and
sing with full awareness of what they are doing stylistically.

A cantor should "begin with the end in mind," a bit of wisdom
borrowed from *The Seven Habits of Highly Effective People* by Stephen
Covey. The imagination is a powerful tool. If we can clearly
imagine what we want to sound like, and believe that we will in
fact produce the sound that we have imagined, we are most of
the way there. It is important to think and to hear each pitch before
we sing it each time we sing, and even more important, to trust
our own possibilities. If inner voices cast doubt, contradict them!
Better yet, silence them. If some old tape tells you, "You'll never
reach that note," say to yourself, "That's not true. I'll reach that note
and then some!" If you hear yourself saying that you are inadequate
in any way, tell yourself that you are capable of things you haven't
dreamed of — because you are.

You have probably been surprised by the sound of your own voice as captured on tape. This is because it is not possible to listen to your own voice with complete objectivity while singing or speaking. We all need to trust other ears for criticism and evaluation of our voices. Tape recordings can be useful, but there are times when a singer must rely on the immediate perception of other people. Seek out a teacher, coach or colleague for this.

Good Habits

Good physical and mental health are essential to good singing. Proper diet and adequate rest are fundamental. Develop a routine of adequate sleep with consistent times for rising and retiring. Extremes of weight in either direction can be a hindrance to singing. Singers should strive for a moderate weight and should engage in some kind of aerobic exercise, no matter how basic. This will improve breathing and will help to develop stamina.

Obviously, singers should not smoke. Caffeine and alcohol are also to be avoided because both of these dehydrate the body and the latter can cause swelling of the vocal bands. Hydration is very important to good singing. In dry weather you may find it helpful to drink as many as ten glasses of water a day.

Singers should be cautious about singing with a cold or any other sickness. The vocal apparatus can become tired and vulnerable to infection. When recovering from a sore throat, use gentle vocalization such as humming for the first few days of practice. Never attempt to sing through pain or irritation. See a throat specialist if such a condition persists.

Singing is a physical activity and the muscles involved in singing should be exercised. Muscular responses should eventually become automatic. Muscle memory can only be developed by repetition and regular practice. Set aside a regular time for daily practice and make it a priority. You will be rewarded with consistent results.

The basics of singing fall into these categories: breathing (respiration), vocal production (phonation), vocal quality and projection (resonance), and articulation (the clear and distinct utterance of words). But before these comes posture.

Posture

Breathing is fundamental to singing and proper posture is fundamental to efficient breathing. Use a full-length mirror to check your posture; ask others to check you when you are performing or when no full-length mirror is available.

Standing with feet no more than shoulders' width apart, distribute your weight evenly on both feet, favoring the balls of your feet. Do not stand flat-footed or rock back on your heels. Your legs should be straight, but your knees should not be locked as this creates tension and can cut off circulation. Stand straight and tall, but not rigid. Your body should be relaxed but not limp. Strive for a feeling of readiness or pleasant anticipation. Imagine that something wonderful is about to happen — maybe it will.

Raise your arms high over your head. Now lower them, keeping your chest high. Keep your back straight, not arched. Your arms should hang naturally at your sides. Your shoulders should be down and back, but in a comfortable position. Do not brace your shoulders back, but let them find the correct position through relaxation. Your neck and head should be straight and in alignment with the rest of the body. Be careful not to tilt the head to either side. Do not jut the head forward or pull it back. It should be balanced over the neck and torso.

> ### Tense?
>
> To eliminate tension, gently roll your shoulders forward several times, and then backward. Let your head drop forward, so that your chin is resting or almost resting on your chest. Slowly roll your head to the left, so that your left ear is toward your left shoulder. Slowly roll your head back to the center, and then to the right. Repeat this several times. Shake out any tension in your arms and legs.

Proper posture should be used in every possible situation so that it becomes completely natural and automatic. A mirror can be used to check posture from time to time, but the feeling of good posture must be memorized. To get the feeling of proper posture, lie down flat on your back on the floor. Make note of your body's alignment. Not only will proper posture help your singing, it will enhance your ability to communicate and help to build your self-confidence.

Breathing

The mechanics of breathing are frequently misunderstood, particularly with regard to the diaphragm. The diaphragm is a dome-shaped muscular membrane attached to the lower portion of the rib cage. It is a partition between the organs of the chest and those of the abdomen. It is the primary muscle of inhalation but is not itself observable.

The diaphragm contracts for inhalation. When it is contracted, it flattens to a lower position, pushing the organs of the abdomen downward and the belly outward. This creates space in the chest cavity and a partial vacuum in the lungs, into which air is drawn. Take a quick, deep breath, as if surprised. Notice the expansion around your waist.

The diaphragm relaxes back up into its dome shape for exhalation. The abdominal muscles assist the diaphragm in controlled relaxation. The abdominal muscles move inward for exhalation, but they should not collapse or be squeezed inward. The resistance of the abdominal muscles to an inward collapse is often referred to as support.

Take a deep breath, and let the air out slowly in a buzz, "zzzzz . . . " (as in zebra). Maintain proper posture throughout, with special care to keep the chest high. Strive for absolute evenness and consistency of sound without accents or interruptions in sound or volume. Repeat the exercise. This time, try to exert a slight outward pressure at the waist while buzzing. The buzz should now have even greater consistency. If not, try lifting a heavy object while buzzing. This will cause the abdominal muscles to contract. The contraction of the abdominal muscles works in opposition to the relaxation of the diaphragm, assisting support.

While some muscle tension is necessary for support, the abdominal muscles must never become rigid or immobile. You must be able to relax, even go limp for inhalation. If these muscles tighten uncontrollably, try lying down and breathing deeply, as in sleep. Panting like a dog is another way to develop and maintain abdominal flexibility.

Another exercise to train the muscles of support is to bend over from the waist, letting your head and arms hang freely. Bend your knees slightly in order to avoid back injury. While in this doubled-

---

Breathing Checklist

Check for the following as you breathe for singing. You should be able to answer "yes" in every case.

- Am I maintaining correct posture throughout?
- Am I allowing my abdomen to move outward for inhalation?
- Am I keeping my head and shoulders still?
- Is my inhalation quiet?
- Am I inhaling within the time allowed by the music?
- Am I able to keep my chest high during exhalation?
- Do my abdominal muscles resist sinking inward too quickly?
- When I sustain a tone, is it even in volume, tone quality and intonation?

over position, take a deep breath and start singing. As you sing, slowly rise to a normal standing position. You may be surprised at the length of phrase you can sustain and the vocal quality you will achieve. This is because the muscles used for standing are also the muscles of support. When you are fully standing and the phrase is completed, stop. Repeat the process singing the next phrase. Regular use of this exercise over a period of weeks or months can dramatically improve support.

Breathe through your nose during long rests to avoid drying the throat and mouth. For short rests and between phrases, breathe through your mouth. This will allow you to take in a large breath quickly, and will open space for vocal resonance.

The following exercises employ rests to assist in teaching proper breathing. Inhale quietly, without gasping. Keep your head and shoulders still for inhalation; check yourself in a mirror. Strive for deep, relaxed inhalation and maintain correct posture throughout.

Of course, your inhalation must happen within the time allowed by the music. Where no rest is provided for a breath between musical phrases, it is a common error to hold the last note of the phrase for its full duration, and then take a breath before beginning the next phrase. This adds time between the phrases and seriously disturbs rhythmic flow. Instead, take a bit of time from the last note of the first phrase to make time for a breath and still arrive on time for the next phrase. See the examples below.

Although the greatest rewards come from proper breathing practiced over months and years, there are other ways to increase breath supply or to use your air supply more efficiently. One way is to inhale and exhale rhythmically to a steady silent count. This is a good way to relate breathing to rhythm, and to train the muscles of respiration. It can be practiced almost anywhere and is very relaxing. Begin by inhaling to a count of four, hold the breath for a count of seven, and exhale for a count of eight. Do not speed up the count during the exhalation. Eventually you will become comfortable and you can even extend the count for the exhalation.

Another way to increase or efficiently use your breath supply is to practice a long phrase by beginning near the end of it, then gradually increasing the portion of the phrase which is sung until you can sing the whole phrase. Be careful not to speed up. You might even divide a long phrase into fractions as shown below. This will give you a goal for your air expenditures — much like a budget.

For ev - er I will sing the good- ness of the Lord.

Pro- claim his mar - vel- ous deeds to all the na - tions.

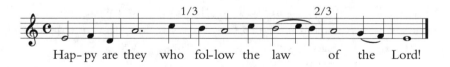

Hap- py are they who fol- low the law of the Lord!

Vocal Production

Sighing and humming are good ways to begin vocalization. The breath should cause the sound to begin. If the vocal chords are closed before exhalation has begun, pressure will build up behind them, causing them to open explosively. This is known as a glottal attack. It results in a much less pleasant sound and can be injurious to the voice over a period of time. To avoid the glottal attack, begin your sighing and humming with an "h" as in "hahhh" and "hmmm."

It is important to begin by warming up with the most beautiful notes in your voice on the most beautiful vowels in your voice. Some people sound better singing "oh" and others "ee." Use a tape recorder and consult others to discover what your best vowel is.

Begin a warm-up using your best vowel in order to establish a high quality of sound as the goal for all of your vowels. Start with a few consecutive notes in a comfortable part of your vocal range and work outward. The vowel [ē] as in "beet" and [ā] as in "paper" are particularly good for achieving clarity of sound. For rounding a strident sound and for adding depth to a thin sound, [ō] as in "oak" is very useful. These vowels should be sung with a pure, consistent vowel sound from beginning to end, unaffected by regional accents.

Vocal Production Test

The following questions should be asked periodically with regard to vocal production:

- Do I begin singing vowels without a glottal attack?
- Do I end a tone with air?
- Do I end a tone with an inhalation?
- Are all of my vowels becoming as beautiful as my best vowels?
- Is my sound consistently beautiful?
- Am I extending my range of beautiful notes?
- Can I move from one pitch to another on a single vowel with a smooth connection of tone, and without sliding?

When practicing a melody to be sung, it is often good to practice singing the entire piece on a single beautiful vowel. After returning to the text, notice which vowel sounds do not match the beauty of the others. Then practice the melody again, substituting a "good" vowel for the problem vowel. Try to substitute vowels which are similar to your problem vowel. You might substitute [ō] as in "oak" for [ŏ] as in "hot," [ā] as in "paper" for [ĕ] as in "letter," [ē] as in "beet" for [ĭ] as in "will," or the reverse of any of these pairs. When you again return to the text, try to keep the tone quality of the substitute vowels.

Most of what is involved in sustaining a tone can be related to proper breathing, but moving from one pitch to another on a single vowel presents other problems. This requires the smoothest possible connection of tones without sliding. It is a common error to aspirate a vowel when moving from one note to another, that is, to insert a superfluous [h] sound at the beginning of the second and subsequent notes of the vowel. The substitution of [y] or [w] for the aspirate [h] may be practiced as a step in correcting this problem, but must be eliminated for actual performance.

Practice the following exercises for smooth movement from one note to another.

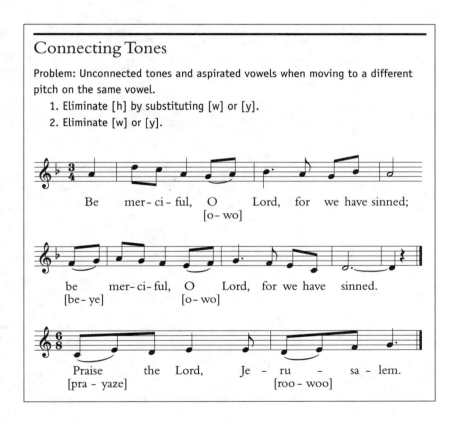

Connecting Tones

Problem: Unconnected tones and aspirated vowels when moving to a different pitch on the same vowel.

1. Eliminate [h] by substituting [w] or [y].
2. Eliminate [w] or [y].

Be mer- ci - ful, O Lord, for we have sinned;
[o- wo]

be mer- ci- ful, O Lord, for we have sinned.
[be- ye] [o- wo]

Praise the Lord, Je - ru - sa - lem.
[pra - yaze] [roo - woo]

The release of a tone should be handled as carefully as the initiation of a sound. Closing the throat is the wrong way to end a tone. Instead, you may continue to exhale, but silently. You may also inhale at the end of a phrase to release a tone. This is a remedy for certain problems of articulation, such as an overly long hiss on a final [s], and it prepares you for the next musical phrase.

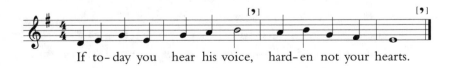

Note that each phrase ends in "s." Shorten the last note of the first phrase in each example in order to provide time for the breath.

The hand of the Lord feeds us; he an-swers all our needs.

Vocal Quality and Projection

Personal taste plays a large role in the tone quality and volume we use for singing. We may imitate those singers we admire, or we may hold preconceived notions about ourselves as a certain "type" of singer. Singers have been known to say such things as "I'm an alto, so I can't sing those high notes," or "I can't sing very loud because I have a light voice." The goal should always be the best sound for a given voice, recognizing that this is highly subjective.

As you practice, be open to new sounds in your voice. Use your imagination. Silence any inner messages that are negative and limiting. Do not be disappointed if you do not sound like your favorite recording artist. The beauty of a voice is its individuality.

I have achieved great results with cantors through role playing. Self-conscious or inhibited singers can imagine that they are confident, extroverted and highly talented singers — someone other than themselves — and achieve incredible results.

Quality and Projection Test

Ask yourself these questions:

- Is my jaw relaxed?
- Is my tongue relaxed and out of my throat?
- Can I feel vibration in my face and mouth when singing?

The quality of their voices can change dramatically and immediately. Each time they serve as cantor they can perform the role of someone else singing until the day when they can see that they have been that person all along.

Vocal resonance is the vibration of air in various chambers, primarily the oral cavity and surrounding areas. It plays a large part in the tone quality of a voice and allows for projection of a vocal sound. Space is needed for resonance. This exercise will demonstrate how important it is. Take a breath, inhaling quickly and deeply, as if surprised. Breathe through your nose and mouth simultaneously. The back of your tongue should be forward and out of your throat. Your throat should feel open without being forced.

Try the exercise again. This time, exclaim "Oh!" immediately after the intake of air. The sound should be rich and full. Trying one last time, sing [ō] as in "oak" immediately after the intake of air. Choose a note in the best part of your voice. Do not back away from the sound. If you have never made this kind of sound before, you may be afraid of it, but it will become familiar over time.

Tension in the jaw and tongue inhibits good vocal quality. The lower jaw should hang freely from the face, and the tongue should lie flat in the mouth with the tip of the tongue just behind the lower teeth. The following exercises will assist in relaxing the jaw and tongue:

- To make sure that the jaw is relaxed, wiggle it with your hand while practicing an exercise.

- Shake your head while singing, as if saying "no," and allow the jaw and tongue to be loose.

- Imagine a heavy weight hanging from your lower jaw that will not allow you to keep your teeth together.

- Make a "dopey" face or adopt a dumbfounded expression.

- Put your hands to the sides of your face to make certain that the back of the jaw is open and relaxed. (There may be tension in the back of the jaw even when the chin is down.)

- To loosen the jaw, exaggerate its movement and say or sing "yah, yah," "wah, wah," "blah, blah," or "gah, gah."

yah, yah, yah, yah, yah,   *etc.*

blah, blah, blah, blah, blah, *etc.*

etc.

- While singing or humming, gently feel the area below your chin. Continue to feel this area without singing. If it bulges when you vocalize, the back of the tongue is stiff and pushed back into the throat. Gently push against this bulge while singing or humming, noting the difference in sound and feeling.

- Stick your tongue out as far as you can and then slowly allow the tongue to return to its normal position without allowing it to roll back into the throat.

- Roll the middle of your tongue forward, up and out of your mouth while keeping the tip down behind the lower teeth. This will give you the feeling of a forward tongue.

- You should be able to change from one vowel to another without moving the jaw. Relax the tongue and allow it to move for the change of vowel.

- Sing through the following exercise, watching in a mirror to ensure that the jaw does not move.

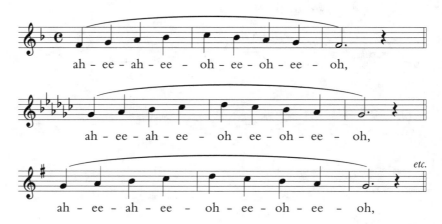

ah – ee – ah – ee – oh – ee – oh – ee – oh,

ah – ee – ah – ee – oh – ee – oh – ee – oh,

etc.

ah – ee – ah – ee – oh – ee – oh – ee – oh,

Some people think of vocal quality and projection as the "placement" of a voice. This is because of physical sensations related to singing, that is, vibration in the head, chest or face. You should strive for a forward placement, a feeling of vibration in the front of the face and mouth. The following exercises should assist you.

- Hum and groan on [n] or [m].

- Imitate a siren on these same consonants.

- Pucker your lips in a "fish mouth" exposing both upper and lower front teeth while singing.

- Imagine a wonderful, awful or strange smell. Then keep that feeling while humming or singing.

- Sneer while singing (for practice only, please).

- Smile inwardly while singing (you may smile outwardly, as well, but not too tightly).

Nasality in the voice is a special problem. It happens when too much air is expelled through the nose. Often the tongue is high in the mouth, forcing the air into the nose. Earlier exercises to loosen the tongue can help. Another exercise is to sing while pinching the nose shut so that you become accustomed to the air moving in the right direction.

Articulation

Americans tend to be careless with the English language, even when singing or proclaiming the word of God. A refrain such as "The Lord is kind and merciful" can sound more like "The Lord is kinda merciful." The phrase "The Lord is my help," takes on quite a different meaning if the final "p" is not carefully attended to.

It is essential that every word of every piece is clearly understood. The goal is always crisp, clear consonants and pure, sustained vowel sounds. There are many fine books that deal in depth with matters of articulation (one example is *The Singer's Manual of English Diction* by Madeleine Marshall, published by Schirmer). This *Handbook for Cantors* will address a few common problems.

One problem involves the differentiation between voiced consonants and unvoiced consonants. Voiced consonants are produced by the voice in coordination with the articulators (the lips, teeth and tongue): for example, [b], [d], [v], [g] and [z]. Unvoiced consonants are produced by the breath in coordination with the articulators, but without the sound of the voice, for example, [p], [t], [n], [k] and [s]. Pronounce these consonants, noting the differences between them. There must be distinct differentiation between [b] and [p], [d] and [t], [v] and [f], [g] and [k], [z] and [s], and other combinations of these voiced and unvoiced consonants.

Final consonants tend to be neglected because care is not taken to sing through to the end of a word. In the case of a final [d], when not followed by a word that begins with a vowel or by any word at all, it is necessary to add a shadow vowel in order for the [d] to be heard as a [d]. (Of course, there are exceptions. When the suffix *-ed* follows an unvoiced consonant, such as [k], it is pronounced [t]. "Looked" is pronounced "lookt.") In the phrase "Hear me, Lord," the word "Lord" should be pronounced "Lorduh" or "Lordih." This is necessary, but it should not be exaggerated. The "uh" or "ih" should barely be heard. Final [b] as in "Job" and final hard [g] as in "beg" are treated the same as final [d], and are given a shadow vowel when not followed by a vowel sound. Read the following lines aloud:

I beg the Lord to forgive me.
Job longed to appear before God.

It is a common mistake to follow other voiced consonants in final position with a shadow vowel. This is unnecessary and only garbles text. "I will praise your name" becomes "I willuh praiseuh your nameuh." Simply sing through [l], [m], [n], [ng], [v] and [z] without adding anything. Shadow vowels are also not necessary to separate words for clarity. One presider was often heard to say, "Let usuh pray" in order to avoid "Let us spray." It would be better to make a slight stop between "us" and "pray."

Sometimes articulation is impaired because the singer diminishes volume on voiced consonants. It is important to sing or hum

---

Articulation Test #1

Tape yourself singing. Listen to the tape and ask yourself these questions:

- When I sing, are final [d]'s, [b]'s and [g]'s distinct?
- Am I adding any unnecessary shadow vowels to the ends of words?
- Do I make clear distinctions between voiced and unvoiced consonants?

"D" and "N," "B" and "M"

Speak and sing the following pairs of words for differentiation between the more "percussive" consonant and the one that is simply voiced.

door — nor
bore — more
day — nay
bay — may
dumb — numb
bum — mum
dud — done
dub — dumb
dear — near
mere — beer

through voiced consonants with loose, relaxed lips and tongue. Carry the intensity of sound to the very end of words and phrases. Sing the refrain "I will praise your name, my King and my God" on a single pitch. Carry the intensity of sound through final [l], [z], [m] and [ng].

It is also important to sing voiced consonants crisply and on one pitch only. Lingering too long over voiced consonants can give improper accents to certain words, and singing a voiced consonant on more than one pitch produces a "slide." Be particularly careful of lingering over [l], [m] and [n], especially when changing pitches. Sing the example below, taking care not to slide.

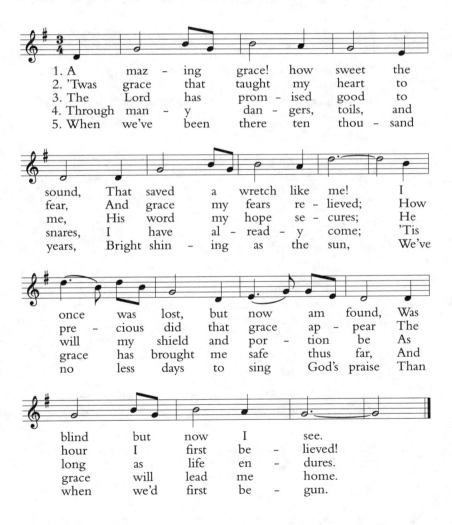

1. A   maz – ing   grace!   how   sweet   the
2. 'Twas   grace   that   taught   my   heart   to
3. The   Lord   has   prom – ised   good   to
4. Through   man – y   dan – gers,   toils,   and
5. When   we've   been   there   ten   thou – sand

sound,   That   saved   a   wretch   like   me!   I
fear,   And   grace   my   fears   re – lieved;   How
me,   His   word   my   hope   se – cures;   He
snares,   I   have   al – read – y   come;   'Tis
years,   Bright   shin – ing   as   the   sun,   We've

once   was   lost,   but   now   am   found,   Was
pre – cious   did   that   grace   ap – pear   The
will   my   shield   and   por – tion   be   As
grace   has   brought   me   safe   thus   far,   And
no   less   days   to   sing   God's   praise   Than

blind   but   now   I   see.
hour   I   first   be – lieved!
long   as   life   en – dures.
grace   will   lead   me   home.
when   we'd   first   be – gun.

Sing the following, using the tip of the tongue and keeping the jaw still, but relaxed. (Use a mirror or your hand to check.) Consonants should be crisp and clean.

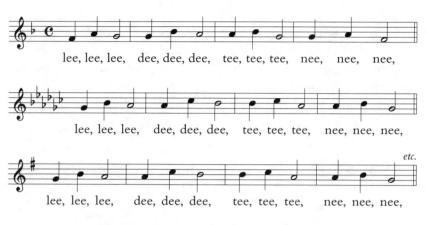

Repeat with other vowel sounds. Sing this next exercise with loose lips and minimal jaw movement.

Singers are often told to sing on the vowel. Vowels sustain a vocal line. It is important not to diminish a vowel sound as it approaches a final consonant, or to allow the approaching consonant to modify the sound of the vowel. English has very few pure vowels, but many diphthongs. Diphthongs are two adjacent vowel sounds: a sustained vowel followed by a quick vowel, such as the combination of "ah" and "ee" in the words "I" and "mine." Both vowel sounds must be pronounced (or the result will resemble a Southern accent), but the first sound should be held as long as possible before singing the second. Of course, the second vowel sound should have the same intensity and volume as the first. Another combination of vowel sounds, a glide, begins with a quick vowel followed by a sustained vowel. "Tuesday," pronounced "Tyoozdaee," has a glide in the first syllable and a diphthong in the second.

In the following musical examples, try singing the underlined diphthongs improperly by moving immediately to the second vowel sound, and then properly by singing on the first vowel sound until the last possible moment.

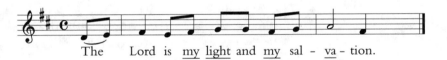

The Lord is my light and my sal - va - tion.

If to-day you hear his voice, har-den not your hearts.

I will praise your name for ev - er, my

king and my God.

Sometimes singers mispronounce vowel sounds, as in "rejoice" (which should be pronounced rĭjois) or "alleluia" (alĕlooya, not alālooya). Refer frequently to a dictionary and the *The Singer's Manual of English Diction*.

The letter [r] presents special problems. When singing in American English, you should use the American [r]. You should not roll or flip an [r] as some Europeans do.

There are times, however, when [r] should be completely omitted: for example, to avoid altering the quality of a vowel that precedes it. When [r] occurs before a consonant, as in "Lord," it does not need to be pronounced to be heard. It is implied. The vowel sound may be left exactly as it is when the [r] is spoken. The letter [r] is also omitted before a pause. An easy shorthand involves a slash through any [r] that is omitted, as in the following.

The Lord is kind and merciful.

An [r] before a vowel sound should be sung. It should be crisp and quick, and should not alter any preceding vowel sound: for example, "spirit" not "spirrrit." Pronounce such an [r] at the beginning of the next syllable, even when doubled, as in "sorrow" (spi-rit, sor-row). Just remember to sing on the vowel.

Study every text you are going to sing and practice reading each text aloud. Be certain of the correct pronunciation of every word; consult a dictionary if necessary. If your articulation is still unclear, try the following:

- Practice whispering the text. It will make you aware of the consonants.

- Sing the text staccato, with each word or syllable as short as possible. This will help you to execute quick consonants.

- Exaggerate your facial movement. This will loosen up the muscles of articulation.

- Sing exaggerated, loud consonants.

The Letter "R"

Practice speaking and singing the following phrases with careful attention to the pronunciation or elimination of [r].

- Let all the earth cry out to God with joy.
- Lord, send out your spi-rit, and renew the face of the earth.
- Lord, you have the words of everlasting life.
- If today you hear his voice, harden not your hearts.

Articulation Test #2

Ask a friend or colleague to listen to you sing and pose the following questions:

- Could you understand every word?
- Did anything in the articulation of the text detract from its meaning or beauty?

FURTHER READING: VOCAL PEDAGOGY

These books offer various degrees of vocal science as well as practical exercises and techniques for singing.

Richard Alderson, *Complete Handbook of Voice Training* (West Nyack NY: Parker Publishing Company, 1979).

Ralph D. Appelman, *The Science of Vocal Pedagogy* (Bloomington IN: Indiana University Press, 1986).

Richard Rosewall, *Handbook of Singing* (Evanston IL: Dickerson Press, 1984).

William Vennard, *Singing: The Mechanism and the Technic* (New York: Carl Fischer, 1967).

Interpretation

This section is for more advanced cantors, but beginners may also find it useful. Incorporate what you can at your present level of ability and experience.

As a singer, you must interpret the words and music you sing to bring a piece to life. You must be able to convey the essence of a piece to the assembly. Of course not every assembly is the same and not every assembly should be addressed in the same way. In the same way, not every celebration is the same. Always keep your particular assembly and celebration in mind when interpreting a piece.

To interpret a piece, you must discern the intentions of the author and the composer. If possible, research the text and the origins of both the text and the music. Begin with the information on the page. Is this a psalm or scriptural quotation? Is it a prayer, an acclamation, a hymn of praise, or something else? Read the text carefully for its content. What is its subject? Sing the piece. What is its mood? Is the purpose of this work to console, to challenge, to inspire, to make petition, to lament or to rejoice? Could it have more than one purpose?

Try to identify the following in the music and words that begin on the next page.

- origin of the text
- origin of the tune
- subject matter
- mood
- liturgical usage

Another guide to the interpretation of a piece is the form of both text and music. Begin with the obvious. Note any textual and musical repetitions, both literal and approximate. Is there a refrain? Do verses have parallel ideas? Is the music the same for each verse, related, or completely different? Does each phrase (musical and textual sentence) have the same number of measures? Notice the phrase structure, as in the example that begins on the next page.

Also, look at the music for delineations of sections by means of double bars, changes of tempo or meter, changes in intensity or dynamic and changes in the instrumental parts.

Identify the textual and musical points of climax. Read the text aloud. Note the words and phrases in the text that are most important to its message. Underline these words in order to emphasize them. In the music, look for extremes of melodic range and for notes emphasized by longer duration. Look for musical accents and for words and phrases emphasized by extremely loud or soft dynamics, or by sudden changes of volume. Note those places where the music best depicts the text (a technique sometimes called text painting).

Look for the following in the example below.

- repetitions or presence of a refrain

- similarity or dissimilarity between verses

- phrase structure

- double bar or change of key

- changes in volume

- high points in text and music

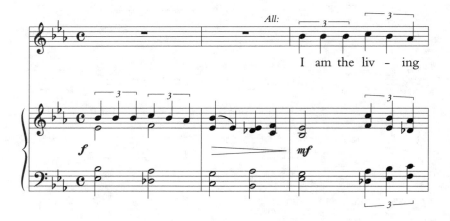

At the most basic level of interpretation, you must bring out important words and phrases. Once you are comfortable with that, you are ready to deal with the interpretation of every word. Just as certain words will be emphasized, other words will be minimized, but there are more than two levels of inflection. Additionally, there are natural word accents. Note the underlined words and syllables in this sentence. Word accents are often undermined by singers. How many times have you heard someone sing "alleluia," simply because that syllable had a longer duration, came on the downbeat, or was given the highest or lowest pitch in a phrase?

Natural word accents must take precedence in order for the text to be clearly understood. Practice by speaking any text you are going to sing, and strive for the same inflection when words and music are put together.

Word color is another way to enhance interpretation. It involves the nuances of saying or singing a text so that its meaning is absolutely clear. It might be thought of as a positive or negative reaction to a word, as a personal image of a word. Explore fully your feelings about texts and try to convey as much as you can in rendering them.

There are other considerations in interpreting a piece. Tempo is important, even if metronome markings have been provided. In a "live" room with a great deal of reverberation and slow decay of released tones, tempo must be slower for nuances in inflection to be heard. Your own ideas about the piece may affect your choice of tempo, but the composer's intent should be respected. Try different tempos to see which best fits the piece.

Your eyes are important in communicating the essence of a piece. Eye contact is particularly effective at the end of a thought. It punctuates what you have to say and actively involves your listeners.

The eyes and face can communicate a wide range of emotions and feelings. Dropping the eyes may indicate shame or sorrow. Raising the eyes just above the heads of the assembly, looking into the distance, may be appropriate for addressing God, although, of course, God is present in the assembly.

Memorize the piece if you can. Keep the assembly in mind as you practice. Draw on your own belief in what you are singing and recall life experiences that help you to relate to the text. Of course, you will have difficult days, days when your mood does not fit your assigned song, and even days when your faith has been shaken. You still have the same responsibilities on such days. You have a duty to no less than the prayer of the church. Use memory or imagination to rejoice when you are sad, to be serious when you feel giddy, and to exhibit faith on days when your faith is weak.

Believe what you are singing, and work to make others believe. Use your face, your eyes and your entire self to do so in a way that is authentic and unaffected. Allow yourself to be personally involved in every song's praise, prayer or lament.

Attending to Words

Try to speak/sing (on a single pitch) the underlined words with as much feeling or meaning as possible.

Lord, let us see your kindness, and grant us your salvation.

Lord, come and save us.

My soul rejoices in my God.

Be merciful, O Lord, for we have sinned.

Out of the depths I cry to you, O Lord.

Let my tongue be silenced if I ever forget you.

Taste and see the goodness of the Lord.

My God, why have you abandoned me?

Like a deer that longs for running streams, my soul longs for you, my God.

Exsultet

The Exsultet is the preeminent chant of cantor repertoire, both because of its difficulty and because of its importance in the liturgical year. Yet very few cantors have ever sung the Exsultet, or have seen printed music for it. (Some have never even heard it!) It is not included in any hymnals or missalettes. It is only available in the sacramentary or as a separate entity. As commonly happens, there is no definitive version of the chant. Even the version in the sacramentary varies from publisher to publisher. Only the text is the same.

The traditional Exsultet is a lengthy song of praise set to chant. It is difficult to execute and, if it is not well done, can be difficult to listen to. Though assigned to the deacon, it may also be sung by a cantor. The decision should be based upon ability: Who can sing it in a way worthy of its poetry and message?

The version included here takes into consideration several preexisting versions, but especially Gregorian chant. (The parts rendered by the priest or deacon are not included.)

In the Solesmes method of interpreting Gregorian chant, notes are arranged in groupings of two or three. The modern notation most commonly used in the "translation" of neumatic Gregorian notation shows single notes following one after another with no indication of these groupings. I have attempted to provide groupings that are true to the earlier notation, in order to encourage the natural ebb and flow of sound that is so essential to the rendition of chant.

Study and practice the Exsultet, not only in this version, but in others as well. Singers and instrumentalists learn a repertoire of arias and concertos far beyond any they will ever get a chance to perform, not only because it prepares them for any opportunity, but because it is essential to their development. This chant has much to teach us. Here are a few suggestions for studying it.

To begin, study the text alone. Remember that diction in singing is different from diction in speech. Consult *The Singer's Manual of English Diction* for more information. Here are some suggestions for pronunciation.

rejoice	rĭ-jois *not* rē-jois
heavenly	hĕ-vĕn-li *not* hĕ-vĭn-li *or* hĕ-vən-li
angels	ān-jĕlz *not* ān-jəlz
our king	au̇-ə king
trumpet	trum-pĕt *not* trum-pət
earth	əth
your king	yȯ king
conquered	kŏn-ku̇d
darkness	däk-nĕs
vanishes	văn-ĭsh-ĕz *not* văn-ĭsh-əz
forever	fȯr-ĕv-ə
mother church	mə-thə chu̇ch
savior	sāv-yȯ
resound	rĭ-zound *not* rē-zound

Next, you might practice the chant melody on a single vowel sound (your best) one section at a time. I would recommend starting with the first four measures as they are presented here. The musical ideas in this section are repeated two more times, so you will have a head start on the next two sections. After you are comfortable with this first section, try adding the text. Watch for those things we should always watch for — singing on the vowel, legato singing without sliding, and of course, excellent intonation.

After you have learned the first three sections, all of which are based on the same musical idea, you will be ready to move on to the section that begins "It is truly right. . . ." Sing the first three measures on a single vowel. This musical idea will be repeated many times with only minimal variation for the remainder of the piece.

Notice the natural section breaks, and any repetitions, as well as the nature of any variations. The variations provide interest, and in many cases serve to underscore the text.

You can sing this chant in any key by beginning on any pitch and keeping the intervals between notes the same as in the printed music. The key provided should work well for most singers.

Chant should be sung with very little vibrato — or at least vibrato of little amplitude. Diction is critical. Let the notes serve the text, not vice versa.

For further insight into the rendition of this chant, examine the evening thanksgiving for Evening Prayer in any season of the liturgical year. I'm sure you will see the similarities.

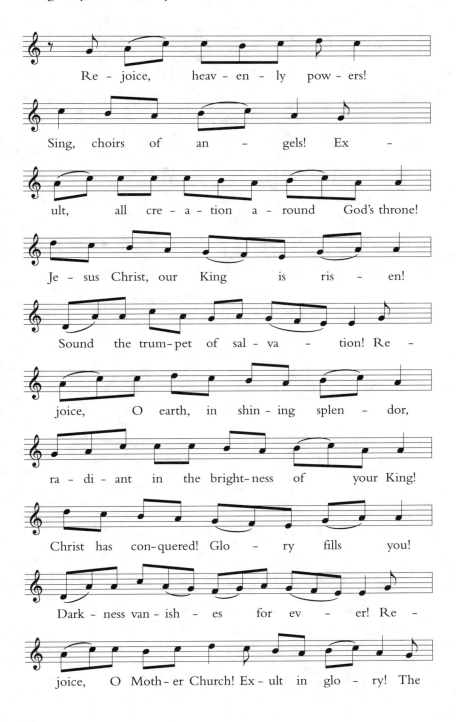

Re - joice, heav - en - ly pow - ers!

Sing, choirs of an - gels! Ex -

ult, all cre - a - tion a - round God's throne!

Je - sus Christ, our King is ris - en!

Sound the trum- pet of sal - va - tion! Re -

joice, O earth, in shin - ing splen - dor,

ra - di - ant in the bright- ness of your King!

Christ has con- quered! Glo - ry fills you!

Dark - ness van - ish - es for ev - er! Re -

joice, O Moth- er Church! Ex - ult in glo - ry! The

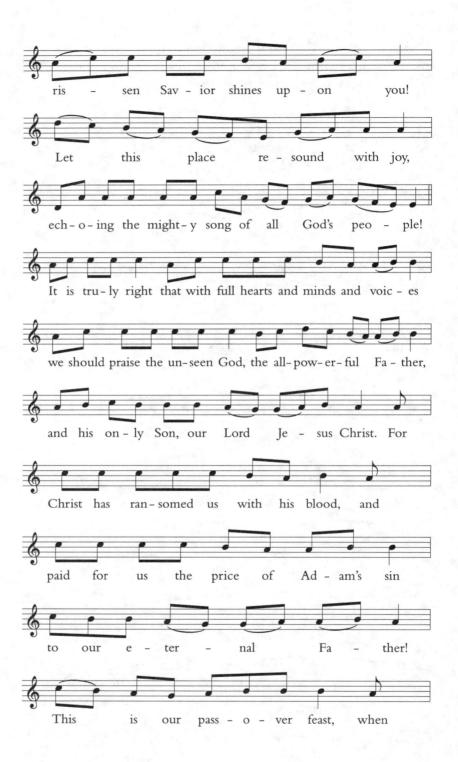

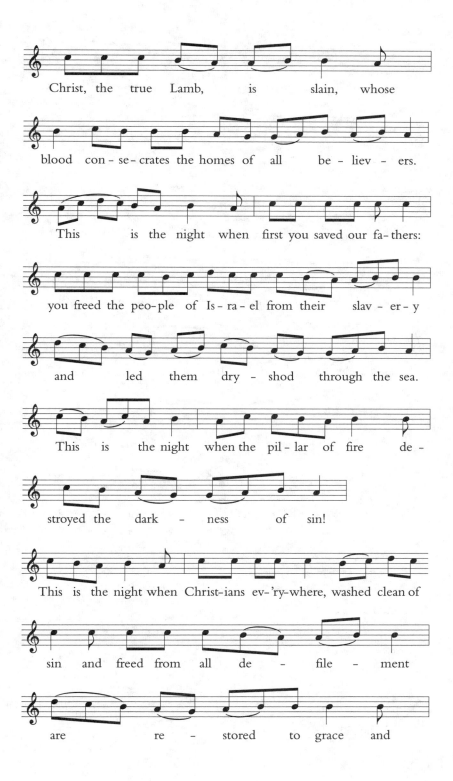

Christ, the true Lamb, is slain, whose
blood con-se-crates the homes of all be-liev-ers.
This is the night when first you saved our fa-thers:
you freed the peo-ple of Is-ra-el from their slav-er-y
and led them dry-shod through the sea.
This is the night when the pil-lar of fire de-
stroyed the dark-ness of sin!
This is the night when Christ-ians ev-'ry-where, washed clean of
sin and freed from all de-file-ment
are re-stored to grace and

grow to - geth — er in ho - li - ness

This is the night when

Je - sus Christ broke the chains of death and

rose tri - um — phant from the grave. What

good would life have been to us, had

Christ not come as our Re - deem - er?

Fa - ther, how won - der - ful your care for us! How

bound - less your mer - ci - ful love! To

ran - som a slave you gave a - way your son. O

hap - py fault, O nec - es - sar - y sin of A - dam, which

gained for us so great a Re - deem - er!

Most blessed of all nights, Cho - sen by God to

see Christ ris - ing from the dead. Of this night

scrip - ture says: "The night will be as clear as day:

it will be - come my light, my joy." The

pow - er of this ho - ly night dis - pels all e - vil,

wash - es guilt a - way, re - stores lost in - no - cence,

brings mourn - ers joy: it casts out ha - tred,

brings us peace and hum - bles earth - ly pride.

Night tru - ly blessed when

heav - en is wed - ded to earth and

man is re - con - ciled with God!

There - fore, heav - en - ly Fa - ther,

in the joy of this night re -

ceive our eve - ning sac - ri - fice of praise, Your

Church's sol - emn of - fer-ing. Ac -

cept this East - er can - dle, a

flame di - vid - ed but un-dimmed, a

pil - lar of fire that glows to the hon - or of God.

Let it min - gle with the lights of heav - en

and con - tin - ue brave - ly burn - ing

to dis - pel the dark - ness of this night!

May the Morn - ing Star which nev - er sets

find this flame still burn - ing:

Christ, that Morn - ing Star, who came back from the dead, and

shed his peace - ful light on all man - kind, your

Son who lives and reigns for ev - er and ev - er. A - men.

Song Leading Revisited

Students in my cantor training sessions sometimes ask me what resources there are for advanced cantors. People who have read the material and attended the workshops, people who have practiced their craft for a number of years, want to know what to do next. They understand that the cultivation of the voice is not in itself the final goal. Neither is the mastery of increasingly complex musical repertoire or fluency in liturgical jargon.

The goal of study and training is the ability to discern what needs to be done and applying the craft to do it. We sing the liturgy, but we need our song to be expressive of all that it is to be human and all that it is to be church. To help us discover how to do this, Alice Parker poses these questions: What happens when people sing informally together at church and other social gatherings? How does it start? How do we learn? What constitutes good leadership? What is the function of song in worship? What makes it successful?

Clearly, we must have something to say — something to share. We need passion. Well-chosen words held lovingly by the cantor are the only thing worthy of the assembly, and the only thing that will draw them into the prayer. The cantor must go to great lengths to get both the words and the meaning across to the assembly. The melody must always serve the text, never the other way around. If every stanza sounds exactly the same, regardless of the text, something is clearly wrong.

Beyond the communication of the text, cantors must have a transparency that is entirely without pretense. After we have prepared, practiced, rehearsed and cultivated a beautiful singing voice, we must leave all of these behind. It is usually obvious when a singer of any ability is thinking about technique and not simply praying the prayer. This is not an excuse for inadequate preparation or training, but quite the opposite. The more vocal control we have, the better equipped we are to do anything that is desired musically or interpretively, including stripping the voice down to utter simplicity. All that can be done should been done before the liturgy. This allows us to stand honestly and humbly before God and one another.

While the music serves the text, a well-chosen melody also has something to say. We must understand the mood of the melody. This is discussed in the chapter on interpretation, which begins on page 67. From what period in music history is the piece derived and from what country? What was the purpose of the song, if any? How was it likely to be sung or played? Is it a chantlike piece where the pitches are primary, or is it a strongly rhythmic piece? To convey what the melody has to say, we must have it in our voices and in our very bones. This means it is either a part of our repertoire — or we have practiced and practiced and practiced!

To effectively teach music to the assembly, use the lining-out method, without accompaniment, described on page 23. Teach by rote so that nothing will come between you and the assembly. Because you are teaching notes, words and rhythms does not mean that your singing should lack expression. Show your love of the piece. Demonstrate for the people the way you wish it to be sung. And always maintain a love and respect for the people with whom you are singing. This will also be conveyed, consciously or unconsciously. Draw people out with subtlety and nuance rather than volume and aggression. Listen to the assembly as intently as possible. This is the hard part. We are used to talking and singing *at* people, not *to* them, and as a society, we are poor listeners.

How do we learn how to teach songs? Dr. Parker's method is wonderful. Students in one of her seminars were instructed to pair off and teach a song to their partner, seated face-to-face in a place off by themselves. She told them to echo back to the one teaching exactly what they had heard. This technique is often used to improve verbal communication. After listening to someone, you echo back to them what you heard them say. If you have heard incorrectly, or if the meaning was skewed, the first one again tries to communicate the message, and the second again repeats what was heard. This is the very thing we did in Dr. Parker's seminar, but in a musical idiom.

Such an exercise has the potential for complete clarity in teaching, and also for great intimacy. It can be a loving exchange of song between two people, leading to a loving exchange of song with an entire assembly. We can sing to one another all the time, to our young and to our old, saying, "Let me teach you a song. Then you teach me one." And just as a writer frequently writes for one other person, we can recall the experience of singing for a single person when we sing for the assembly. How can we hope to achieve anything with an entire assembly if we cannot sing to one person?

The exercise serves another purpose, as well as preparing us to teach. It is a small thing that we can do to keep the experience of singing alive. Singing is so rare in the lives of most people that it has become unnatural and of monumental proportions. Let us all sing, not only for the assembly at Sunday liturgy, but also throughout the week for our friends and loved ones, family and acquaintances, and at every opportunity. And we should always remember to ask, "Now, will you teach me your song?"

I believe much of Alice Parker's work with hymn singing is inspired by the groups that still practice shape-note singing. Shape notes were a kind of notation used in early American hymnody, such as Kentucky harmony. Most of the singing of groups that preserve this tradition is robust (to say the least) and without nuance. Dr. Parker's work is a more refined variation on the theme. In either event, the gathering of people to sing this music, even in an unsophisticated way, is an affirmation of life, and a preservation of both folk music and folk music-making.

Another model to explore in encouraging song among people is the community sing, a practice that flourished during the Great Depression and World War II. Community gatherings were held in public buildings or churches, perhaps on a weekly basis, for the purpose of singing. The repertoire was American folk music — the songs of Stephen Foster, work songs, patriotic songs, and the like. It was not performance — but it was entertainment. People sang to have fun. At the same time, these gatherings built a sense of community, preserved a tradition and allowed everyone to participate equally without being graded or criticized. These gatherings were usually led by a song leader with or without accompaniment. There is some old newsreel footage of Eleanor Roosevelt leading a community sing.

We might borrow from these models. Within our parish communities, we could have regular events where people of all ages are invited to come together just to sing songs and enjoy fellowship. They could be led by song leaders, with or without accompaniment. Here would be a chance to give people real ownership of a musical repertoire. In this way, we might restore some of what has been lost. Song belongs to all human beings as much as it does to the songbirds.

Not all song lends itself to this style of teaching. Hymnody and true folk music usually work the best. What follows is a list of some familiar songs that work well lined-out without accompaniment.

A Mighty Fortress Is Our God (rhythmic setting)
By the Babylonian Rivers
Come, Thou Almighty King
Come, You Sinners, Poor and Needy
Creator of the Stars of Night
God, Who Stretched the Spangled Heavens
God, Whose Almighty Word
How Firm a Foundation
I Sing the Mighty Power of God
Jerusalem, My Happy Home
Jesus Walked This Lonesome Valley
Let All Mortal Flesh Keep Silence
Lord of All Hopefulness
My Shepherd Will Supply My Need
My Song Is Love Unknown
O Sacred Head Surrounded
O Sun of Justice
Of the Father's Love Begotten
Praise the Lord, Ye Heavens Adore Him
Praise to the Lord, the Almighty
Santo, Santo, Santo, Santo
Savior of the Nations, Come
Sing of Mary, Meek and Lowly
Somebody's Knockin' at Your Door
The King of Love My Shepherd Is
There's a Wideness in God's Mercy
Were You There
What Wondrous Love Is This
What Is This Place

FURTHER READING: SONG LEADING

John Bell, *Many and Great* (Chicago: GIA Publications, Inc., 1990). A collection of folk music that lends itself to this kind of rendition.

John Bell, *Sent by the Lord* (Chicago: GIA Publications, Inc., 1991). Another collection of folk music.

Diana Kodner, *Sing God a Simple Song* (Loveland OH: Treehaus Communications, 1995). A book about cantoring and song leading with children. Includes a compact disc of 52 songs appropriate for rituals with children. Available from Liturgy Training Publications or Treehaus.

Alice Parker, *Melodious Accord: Good Singing in Church* (Chicago: Liturgy Training Publications, 1991). A beautiful little book that gathers the wisdom that has enabled Parker to draw song from congregations of all kinds and places.

Yes, We'll Gather! Singing Hymns with Alice Parker (Chicago: Liturgy Training Publications, 1993). A video to invigorate group singing.

When We Sing: Conversations with Alice Parker and Friends (Chicago: Liturgy Training Publications, 1994). A video featuring discussions of why we sing and what we expect of ourselves, texts and tunes when we sing.

The Reason Why We Sing: Community Song with Alice Parker (Chicago: Liturgy Training Publications, 1995). A video for everyone, with a look at song in various groups in many settings.

Practice

The need for regular and routine practice has already been stressed. Once you have established a time for practice, you will need to find a place where you can be free of distractions. It is helpful to have a keyboard instrument to locate pitches. If you do not have access to a piano or organ, inexpensive electronic keyboards are available. If you are not comfortable with a keyboard instrument, use it for pitch references only. The last thing you need is to concern yourself with learning two instruments, voice and keyboard, simultaneously.

There are other important practice tools. A metronome is very useful for tempos and for checking your ability to maintain a steady beat. A full-length mirror is useful for checking posture, the jaw and tongue, and body language. A cassette recorder can help you evaluate your progress. If you have a music stand, use it. You will have greater freedom to practice gestures and a relaxed posture for singing. You may also need your hands to check for such things as a relaxed jaw.

A dictionary of musical terms and notation is essential for anyone who has not studied music and is often helpful for those who have. Many such dictionaries are available (for example, *Elson's Pocket Music Dictionary* by Louis C. Elson, published by Oliver Ditson Company).

The first thing to do in a practice session will depend on what you have already done that day. If you have not yet sung, you should begin with gentle vocalization, such as humming, sighing aloud, whimpering and groaning. Begin in the lower to middle portion of your range (your range is the entire compass of notes that you can comfortably sing). If you are more comfortable with descending scales, begin with a five-note descending scale. If you prefer, use an ascending scale. In either case, transpose the figure upward or downward by half-steps, as in the example on the next page.

Whenever you vocalize, practice proper posture. Be certain that your face is relaxed and that your lips are loosely together for humming. You should feel a buzzing sensation at the front of your mouth and even in parts of your face. Do not attempt to hum too high in your range, past what is comfortable. Strive for a smooth, even, connected sound. Experiment with both [m] and [n]. These will produce slightly different effects for different people. If you are having trouble in achieving a forward buzzing sensation, try [n]. If your voice is generally nasal, that is, if you sound as if you sing and talk through your nose, use an [m].

Any variation on the five-note pattern might be your next step. Some examples are provided below. To continue, incorporate humming with a vowel sound. Use [n] or [m] and combine it with your best vowel.

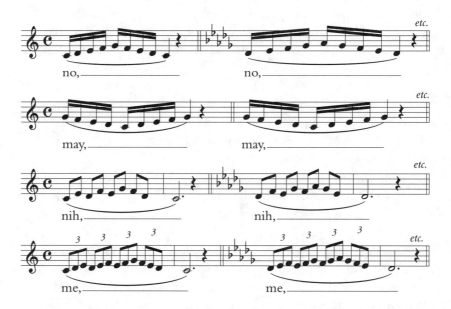

Scales and other melodic patterns are not merely mindless exercises allowing us to focus on the voice. They are important because they are the very components of the music we sing. Children learn the alphabet before learning to read, just as musicians learn individual notes, but actual reading is grasping combinations of letters that form words and words that form phrases. Musicians need to be able to mentally hear and to physically sing various arrangements of notes, musical motives and phrases, relating note to note in myriad ways.

The amount of time to spend on gentle vocalization will vary from one person to another. As your voice becomes accustomed to singing, put more energy behind it. You should not force the voice, but if you do not use it to its capacity, you will never become vocally strong. Allow at least fifteen minutes for the warm-up described thus far. This can also be your vocal warm-up prior to a liturgy or rehearsal. You can include any other exercises that are helpful to you and that address a problem in your singing, such as breathing or articulation.

The next step in your practice session involves the music that you are working on for your ministry. If you are going to practice several pieces, begin with the easiest and work through to the most difficult. Otherwise you might abandon good vocalization for the sake of overcoming other difficulties of musicianship and interpretation.

> ### Practice Session
>
> 1. Sigh, whimper, groan and hum to warm up the voice.
> 2. Continue with five-note descending or ascending scales.
> 3. Incorporate singing and vary the pattern of the scale.
> 4. Move to exercises addressing your specific vocal problems.
> 5. Practice your music, beginning with the easiest pieces.

Begin by singing the piece on a single vowel, your best. If the piece is long or unfamiliar, you might break it down into sections. Modify the vowel sound as needed in the extremes of your range. In other words, when singing very high or very low in your range, alter the vowel sound slightly to maintain consistent sound and ease of production. As a rule, the higher you sing, the more open the vowel sound needs to be. The hymn *Amazing Grace* has the familiar phrase "saved a wretch like *me*," with "me" being the highest pitch. In good singing, the vowel is modified toward [i] as in "mint."

Next, speak the piece in rhythm, or chant it in rhythm on a single pitch. Particular care must be given to crisp and clear articulation.

Now put together the text and tune by singing the piece as written. Try to note any problems or difficulties as you go. Stop and mark them in the music. Things to watch for include:

- running out of air
- pitch problems
- difficulties of range
- vowel sounds which are less beautiful than your best
- sliding between pitches or when starting a phrase (scooping).

In striving for consistency of sound, match all sounds to your best sound. It is a common error to modify a truly beautiful vowel or pitch in order to match it with the rest of the voice, which may not yet be as beautiful.

Having found any rough spots in the music, now focus your attention on them. These problems should be removed from the context of the music and practiced slowly and carefully. If you continue to go over a musical passage without correcting flaws, you are actually solidifying them. Rectify problems one by one before restoring these excerpts to the context of the music.

Go through the piece on the next page as if you were working on it for your own ministry. The numbers below refer to particular places in the music.

1. Look out for accidentals. (An accidental is a flat, sharp or natural that occurs independently of the key signature.)

2. Be careful of intonation for this "leap."

3. Be careful not to go flat in descending patterns.

4. Be careful not to run out of air.

5. Be careful to sing legato, connected.

Practicing a Piece

1. Divide the piece into phrases or small sections.
2. Hum and sing sections on a single vowel until comfortable.
3. Speak the text in rhythm or chant it on a single pitch.
4. Combine text and tune, still practicing small sections.
5. Isolate and concentrate on problem areas.
6. Return problem sections to the context of the piece and practice larger sections.
7. Sing through the piece in its entirety.
8. Continue to work on the piece for interpretation.

Cantor, then all

Cleanse us, O Lord, from all our sins:

wash us, and we shall be clean, clean as new

snow. snow. I will pour clean wa - ter

o- ver you and wash a- way all your sins. snow. A new

heart will I give you, says the Lord.

The length of your practice session will depend on the size of your task and the endurance of your voice. It will probably be necessary to rest your voice briefly during a practice session. Use these breaks to mark your music and to think about body language, gestures and interpretation. When your voice becomes very tired you should stop. You may want to divide your practice into two daily sessions of shorter duration. At any rate, your practice should last from fifteen minutes (after warming up) to an hour.

Whether a song is learned by ear or by sight-reading, every sound must be heard internally — in the memory or the imagination — before it can be produced. Apart from regular practice, ear training can and should be approached in a concentrated way. Cantors can begin by teaching themselves to sing intervals in tune. Select a pitch, and then carefully move a half-step from that note in either direction. Sing an [n] followed by a closed vowel such as the [e] in "me" or the [a] in "may." (Avoid beginning with open vowels such as the [o] in "God" or the [e] in "met.") When this is under control, you can try other vowels. Then select another pitch and repeat the process, always beginning with closed vowel sounds and moving later to open ones. You might spend an entire week on half-steps. Then move on to whole steps.

Although vibrato is inherent in singing, this kind of work should be done without it, singing with straight tones as much as possible. When I was in college, our ear-training classes were full of singers who could perform the exercises with a beautiful sound and well-modulated vibrato — but too often out of tune.

Continue your work through all the intervals: major and minor thirds, sixths and sevenths and perfect fourths and fifths. If you need to, you can find these intervals notated in music theory books and take them to a keyboard, but those who can should work without instruments as much as possible. Over time you will be able to sing intervals better in tune, and if you train your eye to recognize intervals in your music, your sight reading will also improve.

It is also important to develop the ability to match pitches as closely as possible. There is a wonderful game at the Museum of Science and Industry in Chicago in which a pitch is briefly sounded electronically and the listener has to quickly reproduce that pitch as closely as possible by turning a dial. The computer tells the player how close he or she was to the actual pitch. (If A=440 is played, the player may generate A=443 or A=437.) Along the same idea, the electronic tuning devices used by many guitarists could be beneficial to singers wanting to develop the ability to accurately match pitches. The needle will show you when you are singing a given pitch precisely. Again, much of this work should be done with straight tones. The most reliable method for matching pitches without electronic devices is to listen for "beats" between the two pitches involved. (If you have not experienced this phenomenon, drop in some time when the church's piano or organ is being tuned.) This kind of tuning cannot be done with vibrato. Orchestral instruments that are played with vibrato are frequently tuned without vibrato. The oboist sounding the orchestral "A" for tuning will begin with a straight tone. Of course, singers must also cultivate matching pitches with the use of vibrato.

Incidentally, those with perfect pitch will have to work to overcome this gift when instruments are pitched at something other

---

Practicing a Piece with Others

1. Check for introductions, interludes and any added time between stanzas or verses.

2. Check for balance between the voice and the instruments in the acoustical environment of the worship space.

3. Check for agreement in rhythmic precision and consistency of tempo. (To rectify problems, you can remove them from the context of the music. For practice purposes, try the following: Slow the tempo; speed the tempo; clap, speak or chant the rhythm; try a staccato or very short style of execution.)

4. Check for intonation problems. Ask yourself these questions if you are having difficulties. Do I lack support? Am I running out of air? Is there tension in my jaw or tongue? Am I maintaining proper posture? Am I sustaining energy through long notes and phrases? Do I overshoot descending or ascending lines? Am I struggling with the difficulty of the piece? Do I need to compensate for an acoustical space that is dull? Have I had adequate rest? Am I having difficulty hearing the instruments? Are the instruments out of tune?

than A=440, or in order to tune with certain notes that are out of tune on an instrument. Perfect pitch is actually perfect pitch memory, much like total recall or photographic memory. The standardization of pitch to A=440 is a fairly recent development in music history (as well as a Western phenomenon). It is more important to be in tune with others than to be right by such standards.

There are some basic principles to keep in mind that will assist you in maintaining good, consistent intonation.

PROBLEMS INHERENT IN THE MUSIC

- When singing repeated notes, it is easy to go flat. Think carefully about each consecutive note.

- Descending lines also have a tendency to go flat. Be careful not to overshoot descending intervals.

- When singing the interval of a major third, make sure the upper note is high enough. This is another common problem, even among accomplished musicians.

PROBLEMS INHERENT IN SINGING

- Ends of phrases and sustained notes can go out of tune because of lack of support, which sends the note flat, or too much support, pushing the note too high. Listen carefully at the ends of phrases and through long held notes.

- Singers often try to "feel" pitches in the voice. This is not a reliable method for singing in tune. One must always listen. It is important, if not essential, to "hear" the note in one's head before it is actually sung.

- Careful attention should be given to voiced consonants, such as [l], [m] and [n], so that there is no sliding into pitches. Most singers are not even aware that they do this.

- Intonation problems can result from tension in the jaw or tongue. See "The Cantor as a Singer," which begins on page 47, for exercises to remedy these.

- Vibrato should span an equal distance, not more than a quarter tone, above and below the pitch to be in tune.

- Singers sometimes have difficulty singing in tune in certain parts of their range — extremely high or low notes, or when changing from one register of the voice to another.

This is a matter of technique. Practice problem areas out of the context of the piece, slowly and carefully.

- Loud singing is more frequently out of tune than is soft singing simply because the performer stops listening and takes his or her own voice as the correct pitch, since it is more prominent than anything else.

- Sometimes when cantors are tired, they will sing flat because they do not support the breath. If you are not well rested, pay particular attention to your posture and breathing.

ACOUSTICAL CONCERNS

- In very reverberant rooms, the decaying sound will be slightly lower in pitch than the initial sound because of the Doppler effect. In the Doppler effect, an approaching siren gets higher in pitch as it nears and lower as it moves away into the distance. Singers should be aware of the Doppler effect in certain worship spaces, listening for the initial articulation of pitch rather than pitch of the decaying sound.

- It can sometimes be difficult to hear other instruments or voices. This may be due to a poor acoustical space, placement too far from other musicians or poor registration of the organ. Cantors should make it known that they are having difficulty in hearing, and adjustments should be made to improve these situations.

- A dead acoustical space or low ceiling will sometimes cause singers to go flat. Awareness can help remedy the problem. Improving the space is an even better idea. If the cantor has to fight the space, the assembly will have the same problem.

POOR INTONATION IN OTHERS

- Sometimes the response of the assembly to a cantor intonation, such as the initial statement of a refrain, or the assembly's refrain following a cantor verse, will be flat. Even if the music is unaccompanied, the cantor should attempt to return to the proper tonal center for subsequent verses; otherwise, the pitch can continue to descend until it becomes a congregational growl.

- Too frequently the instruments are so out of tune as to destroy any chance that the cantor will sing in tune. All instruments should be carefully tuned and maintained.

There is no substitute for practice. There are no shortcuts in practice, either, but there are ways to make your practice both more efficient and more enjoyable.

When I was a child, I was as reluctant to practice my music as any other child who doesn't want to put down her toys, so I would come up with little efficiencies a day or two before my lessons — going through my music, finding the rough spots, and then practicing those until they were smooth. I would also ask my mother, a wonderful musician, to coach me. In this way, not only did I get the encouragement of an expert, but I got to spend some quality time with Mom. I eventually came to love practicing as much as performing—and that should be a goal for all of us. I would keep on practicing even if it were the only music-making I ever did.

If practice is something you avoid, think about the reasons why. Find a teacher, coach or accompanist to keep you on the right track. Schedule your practice times just as you would a rehearsal or a liturgy. A pleasant and practical environment for your practice is an added incentive—there's nothing like practicing in a reverberant room! And keep in mind that all music-making, even practice, is a wonderful gift from a loving God.

Related Concerns

Much has been said here about the cantor's craft, but we still need to ask about this ministry: What is it and what is it not? How does the cantor's ministry fit with the other ministries of the church, with the community at large, and with the rest of the cantor's own life as an individual, as a member of a family, and as a member of the body of Chirst?

When Is a Cantor Not a Cantor?

It should be clear by this point that the cantor is not just someone who pops out from the choir. Choir members have their own ministry, which is related to, but not the same as, the ministry of the cantor. With special training and preparation, a choir member could become a cantor, but not all choristers are cantor material. Similarly, the cantor is not just any vocal soloist who comes along, paid or volunteer. Certain gifts of communication and spirituality should be evident in anyone who serves as a vocal soloist in the church. The ministry of the cantor involves an ongoing commitment to the assembly, a commitment to their sung participation and to their prayer.

The cantor does not double as the organist. If an organist is able to serve as a cantor, this is a blessing, but one does not serve as cantor from behind an organ console. It would be better to stand before the assembly and sing without accompaniment. It is our duty to invite many people to the variety of music ministries available, even though it sometimes seems easier for one person to do everything.

Like other ministries, the ministry of the cantor is unique. It requires special gifts and a great deal of commitment. It is a musical, liturgical and pastoral ministry that is both rooted in tradition and thoroughly modern.

The Cantor and Others

The cantor's ministry is distinct but not independent of other ministries. From time to time cantors must evaluate how they work with other ministers and with the community in general. As in any relationship, communication is essential. Ask yourself the following questions:

INTERACTING WITH OTHERS   How do I interact with other members of the community? Do I keep to myself, do I interact with the people I like or do I try to open myself up to interaction with the community as a whole, even to confrontation?

How do I interact with other ministers of music? Am I competitive, excessively demanding or uncharitable? Am I self-righteous? Am I supportive and affirming? Do I feel supported and affirmed? How do I deal with conflict? Am I indifferent to the ministry of others or do I feel a kinship through our common ministry?

How is musical and liturgical preparation accomplished in our community and how do I fit in? Do I make decisions by myself or in consultation with others? Does someone else make these decisions? Am I interested in the process, am I indifferent or do I have strong feelings about it? What are my feelings based on? How do I make my feelings known?

What relationship do I have to those who preside at liturgy? Have I had an opportunity to get to know the presiders? Do I feel at odds with any presider, and if so, why? How do I deal with these feelings? Do I feel supported and affirmed by presiders, and do I offer support and affirmation?

CANTORING AND MY LIFE   Do I think of my ministry only in terms of some portion of my life or do I live my life in the context of my ministry? Do I conduct myself in a way that is appropriate to my public ministry?

Do I take ample time for prayer or am I too busy? How do I keep Sundays and the various liturgical seasons? Do I observe the seasons only in the context of Sunday liturgy, or do I keep certain days of the season (such as the Fridays of Lent)? Am I conscious of the seasons as a way of guiding my life and prayer?

Do I attend weekly liturgy only when I am scheduled as cantor, or do I worship with the community on a weekly basis throughout the year? Is Jesus at the core of my life and ministry?

How do I take care of myself? Is all of my free time spent in the service of the church? Am I using my ministry to avoid family commitments and relationships? Am I unable to say "no" to any request for service? Am I heading for ministerial burnout? What are my true motives for ministry?

Beyond Sunday Morning

It is also good to examine how the various sacraments and rites of the church are celebrated in your parish and what role the cantor plays. Too often, weddings, funerals and baptisms are not treated as communal celebrations of the parish but as private events. Vocal soloists are used at these occasions more often than cantors, if there is music at all. The assembly is rarely invited to sing. Cantors are most needed in situations where people are least likely to sing of their own accord. Communal singing can and should be a part of these celebrations.

A cantor should take time before the beginning of these liturgies to introduce congregational materials and to elicit initial responses from the assembly. Congregational materials should be simple and well known. It is not necessary that everything be sung, but certainly the responsorial psalm and gospel acclamation should be sung as a part of any liturgy of the word. For eucharistic liturgies, the "Holy, holy," the memorial acclamation and the great "Amen" should be sung. Beyond this, choose from appropriate songs, hymns and psalms that are well known or easy to enter into. A good resource for weddings is *Handbook of Church Music for Weddings* by Mary Beth Kunde-Anderson and David Anderson, published by Liturgy Training Publications. *Blest Are Those Who Mourn* is a collection of music for funerals published by GIA Publications, Inc.

Preparation with Other Liturgical Ministers

For all celebrations, large and small, the cantor must be prepared. But this does not apply to the cantor alone. Preparation and even rehearsal should include all the liturgical ministers involved in a celebration. Some of this preparation is individual, but there are points at which ministries interact or merge.

Those involved in a celebration as cantor, lector, presider, acolyte, deacon, eucharistic minister and any others should come together to discuss and even to walk through the specific celebration. The Sunday liturgy during Ordinary Time should be carefully learned by all ministers as individuals and as an ensemble.

Variations in this order for Advent, Christmastime, Lent and Eastertime will need reminders and rehearsals each year. Walking through the liturgy is especially important in the case of once-a-year liturgies, such as those of the Triduum. If ministers are unwilling to come together for this purpose, they need to be reminded that in the liturgy we are not invited to do our own individual thing. We do the Christian community's thing. Instruction sheets and memos are useful, but successful liturgy does not simply spring from the head. It must be in the very bones of those who bear its awesome responsibility.

The cantor cannot determine how other ministers will conduct themselves but can model a way of doing ministry. Neither success nor failure is in your hands. Simply allow yourself to do God's and the church's good but humble work.

Questions for Annual Ministry Review

- Are you willing and able to better your craft?
- Are you willing to be critiqued in matters that affect the performance of your ministry, and hence, the prayer of the assembly?
- Are you willing to contribute the amount of time needed to better your craft?
- What restrictions do you place on your willingness to serve?
- Can you adapt to changes in repertoire and in modes of rendition?
- If opportunities to serve as cantor or soloist for weddings and funerals are lean, does this adversely affect your attitude toward your ministry?
- If you feel competitive with other cantors, might it interfere with performance of your ministry?
- Are you willing to work through problems with other ministers toward ongoing reconciliation?
- Do you need a break from this ministry?

Inclusive Language

The texts that a cantor sings may present special problems. Many people have become sensitive to the preponderance of masculine language and imagery found in the liturgy of the church. While traditional hymns have been reworked and new songs have been written with this sensitivity in mind, the designated texts of the liturgy are not as easily changed. The church continues to struggle with new translations of the psalter, of various prayers and of all of scripture, but the process is long. It involves the consultation and collaboration of biblical scholars, poets, theologians, liturgists and liturgical musicians.

The sung texts of the liturgy should not be changed arbitrarily by anyone who feels inclined to do so. The poetry of the language can easily be lost. Even the changing of hymns and song texts must be handled carefully and on an individual basis.

There are times when language can and should be changed. Such changes should be carefully thought out in consultation with others. Pastoral concern, and not politicizing the liturgy, should determine the changes. Pastoral considerations must be inclusive of the entire community. Alongside the need for language that expresses the equality of all people in the eyes of God, consider the need in ritual for familiarity and consistency.

The pastoral judgment does not stand alone. It must be considered with musical and liturgical appropriateness. The musical judgment would require an appropriate union of text and music. The liturgical judgment would raise questions of symbolic and theological integrity. All three judgments require intelligibility of text. An approach that considers the liturgy in this way will lead to positive and long-lasting changes in the language of worship.

Spirituality

If liturgy is the source and summit of our Christian lives, what should our lives look like? As baptized Christians, we are called to be people of prayer. As cantors, we are leaders of prayer and public ministers of the word. It would seem to be important, then, that we be intimately familiar with prayer, psalmody and the lectionary.

It is important to develop a life of prayer that extends beyond our liturgical celebrations. For those who were Catholic before the Second Vatican Council, the admonition might have been (and might still be) to pray in common as well as in private. For the busy liturgical minister of the present day, the admonition is to pray in private as well as in common. This might begin with taking time on a regular basis to pray the psalms, to dwell on the Sunday scriptures and to cultivate a sense of intercessory prayer. In time, a relationship with God so nurtured and developed will enhance the capacity of a cantor for public ministry, for, in the words of John Mogabgab, "dwelling with God in the intimacy of prayer causes us to grow into the likeness of the One (the God) with whom we share love. As this happens, the psalmist's experience will become our own" (*Weavings,* Vol. IV, No.2, March/April 1989). Liturgy Training Publications offers books to assist in personal as well as communal prayer, many of which are related to the lectionary and the liturgical year. This can be helpful in helping liturgical ministers to integrate the church's calendar with their own.

We can and should pray with the psalms. They constitute a large and significant body of the material for which we are responsible as cantors. Beyond this, the psalms can teach us how to speak before God, embracing all the passions and moods and conditions of humankind, and hence, our own. *Psalms for Morning and Evening Prayer* is an excellent resource for praying the psalms. *Proclaim Praise* has fewer psalms, but provides the other essential parts for a simple celebration of morning or evening prayer. Praying the psalms upon rising, before sleep and at mealtime can easily become the ritual practice of a home, once a commitment is made.

In addition to praying with the psalms, one can and should pray with other scriptures. *Prayers for Sundays and Seasons* offers an introduction to *lectio divina,* or holy reading. Lectionary readings, preceded by the collect of the day, are read prayerfully until a word or phrase takes on special significance. The reading is then meditated upon, or murmured much the same way one meditates in murmuring the rosary. In the next stage, we speak to God in our own words or using the scriptural prayers or intercessions provided. The prayer concludes in quiet contemplation. The fruit of the prayer might be a word or phrase returned to again and again throughout the day as a way of restoring focus and purpose.

Many people enthusiastically endorse journaling as a means of prayer. Such prayer can be lectionary-based, and should be done regularly to be effective. *Listening to God's Word* was created for children and parents to do just that. In addition to the Sunday scriptures, it includes related questions, activities, stories, poems, games, play and prayer.

Intercessory prayer is a familiar form of prayer appropriate to both public and private worship. Like all prayer, intercession begins with our recognition of God's love and care for us. Our intercession is joined to that love and care. Beyond serving as an entrance into relationship with God, intercession affects the one who prays in several ways. Douglas Steere, an expert on the contemplative life, wrote in *Weavings,* Vol. IV, No. 2, March/April 1989, what is for me the best explanation of intercessory prayer:

> Whether we intend to or not, to pray for another is to become involved in his or her life. . . . Apart from the psychic cost of this vulnerable involvement for others, in most cases to pray for others almost inevitably involves us in physical responsibilities for them, whether we meant to do that or not. [This] may consist of time for visits, gifts of food, books, letters and often many forms of physical support. A further cost of very different character that intercession almost inevitably exacts is the searching of the life of the one who prays and the bidding that comes to that person for deeper abandonment in their own life. All too swiftly we discover that it is not what we have already given away to God that makes us suffer but a matter of what we are still holding back from God. And we find it harder

and harder to ask for changes in others without a willingness to yield to God whole new areas of off-limits territory in our own life. In the end, our intercessions are likely to become more and more "Thy will be done. . . . "

The commitment to a life of prayer can nurture and sustain us in our ministry, but moreover, can convert, enlighten and transform us. If we cannot or will not do this for ourselves, how can we hope to do this for others?

FURTHER READING: SPIRITUALITY

Eileen Drilling and Judy Rothfork, *Listening to God's Word* (Chicago: Liturgy Training Publications, annual).

Gabe Huck, editor, *Prayers of Those Who Make Music* (Chicago: Liturgy Training Publications, 1981).

Gabe Huck, editor, *A Sourcebook about Liturgy* (Chicago: Liturgy Training Publications, 1994).

ICEL, *Psalms for Morning and Evening Prayer* (Chicago: Liturgy Training Publications, 1995).

Diana Kodner and Alan Hommerding, editors, *A Sourcebook about Music* (Chicago: Liturgy Training Publications, 1997).

Melissa Musick Nussbaum, *I Will Arise This Day* (Chicago: Liturgy Training Publications, 1996).

Melissa Musick Nussbaum, *I Will Lie Down This Night* (Chicago: Liturgy Training Publications, 1995).

Peter J. Scagnelli, *Prayers for Sundays and Seasons* (Chicago: Liturgy Training Publications, annual).

Music Acknowledgments

The English translation of the psalm responses and Lenten gospel acclamations from the *Lectionary for Mass* © 1969 International Committee on English in the Liturgy, Inc. (ICEL); excerpts from the English translation of the *Rite of Funerals* © 1970 ICEL; the English translation of the Exsultet (Easter Proclamation) from the *Rite of Holy Week* © 1972 ICEL; excerpts from the English translation of the General Instruction of the Roman Missal from *The Roman Missal* © 1973 ICEL; the English translation of the Canticle of the Lamb and the antiphon "As morning breaks" from *The Liturgy of the Hours* © 1974 ICEL; music from *Music for the Rite of Funerals and Rite of Baptism for Children* © 1977 ICEL; music for the Canticle of the Lamb from the *Resource Collection of Hymns and Service Music for the Liturgy* © 1977 ICEL; music by Willcock and Mews for psalm refrains from *ICEL Lectionary Music: Psalms and Alleluia and Gospel Acclamations for the Liturgy of the Word (r)* © 1982 ICEL; the music and text of the Canticle of Mary and Canticle of Zechariah from *The Liturgical Psalter* © 1994 ICEL. All rights reserved.

Page 14. "We remember." Marty Haugen. Copyright © 1980 GIA Publications, Inc., Chicago. All rights reserved.

Page 15. "Eat this bread." Text: John 6, adapted by Robert Batastini and the Taizé Community. Music: Jacques Berthier. Copyright © 1984 Les Presses de Taizé (France), used by permission of GIA Publications, Inc., exclusive agent. All rights reserved.

Page 23. "At the name." Music: Ralph Vaughan Williams, 1872–1958. Copyright © 1931 *Enlarged Songs of Praise*. Reprinted by permission of Oxford University Press.

Page 26. "Sing to the Lord." Music: Douglas Mews. Copyright © ICEL.

Page 26. "The Lord is near." Music: Christopher Willcock. Copyright © ICEL.

Page 26. "The Lord is near." Music: Douglas Mews. Copyright © ICEL.

Page 26. "Hear us, Lord." Music: Christopher Willcock. Copyright © ICEL.

Page 30. "In the silent hours. " Psalm 134. Text: ICEL. Music: Howard Hughes, sm. Copyright © 1986 GIA Publications, Inc., Chicago. All rights reserved.

Page 34. "Alleluia, alleluia." Canticle of the Lamb, Revelation 19:1 – 7. Music: Howard Hughes, sm. Copyright © ICEL.

Page 35. "Jesus is the image." Colossians 1:12 – 20. Music: Robert LeBlanc. Copyright © 1986 GIA Publications, Inc., Chicago. All rights reserved.

Page 36. "I will praise." Refrain: copyright © ICEL. Psalm 63: New American Bible, copyright © 1969, 1970 Confraternity of the Christian Doctrine. Music for psalm: copyright © 1984 Richard Proulx.

Page 37. "As morning breaks." Music: Howard Hughes, sm. Text: Copyright © 1959 Ladies of the Grail (England), used by permission of GIA Publications, Inc., exclusive agent. All rights reserved.

Page 38. "My shepherd." Psalm 23. Music: Joseph Gelineau. Copyright © 1959 Ladies of the Grail (England), used by permission of GIA Publications, Inc., exclusive agent. All rights reserved.

Page 50. "The Lord has done." Music: Joseph Roff. Text: ICEL. Copyright © 1984 World Library Publications, Inc., a division of J.S. Paluch Company, Inc., 3825 N. Willow Rd., Schiller Park IL 60176. All rights reserved. Used with permission.

Page 50. "I received." Copyright © 1986 GIA Publications, Inc., Chicago. All rights reserved.

Page 51. "For ever I will sing." Music: J. Robert Carroll. Text: ICEL. Copyright © 1975 GIA Publications, Inc., Chicago. All rights reserved.

Page 51. "Proclaim his marvelous deeds." Music: R. Currie. Text: ICEL. Copyright © 1986 GIA Publications, Inc., Chicago. All rights reserved.

Page 51. "Happy are they." Music: Richard Proulx. Copyright © 1986 GIA Publications, Inc., Chicago. All rights reserved.

Page 52. "For ever I will sing." Music: Robert E. Kreutz. Text: ICEL. Copyright © 1984 World Library Publications, Inc., a division of J.S. Paluch Company, Inc., 3825 N. Willow Rd., Schiller Park IL 60176. All rights reserved. Used with permission.

Page 52. "I will praise." Music: David Haas. Text: ICEL. Copyright © 1983 GIA Publications, Inc., Chicago. All rights reserved.

Page 53. "Be merciful." Music: Marty Haugen. Text: ICEL. Copyright © 1986 GIA Publications, Inc., Chicago. All rights reserved.

Page 53. "Praise the Lord." Music: James M. Burns. Text: ICEL. Copyright © 1971 World Library Publications, Inc., a division of J.S. Paluch Company, Inc., 3825 N. Willow Rd., Schiller Park IL 60176. All rights reserved. Used with permission.

Page 55. "If today." Music: David N. Johnson. Text: ICEL. Copyright © 1984 World Library Publications, Inc., a division of J.S. Paluch Company, Inc., 3825 N. Willow Rd., Schiller Park IL 60176. All rights reserved. Used with permission.

Page 56. "The hand." Music: David N. Johnson. Text: ICEL. Copyright © 1984 World Library Publications, Inc., a division of J.S. Paluch Company, Inc., 3825 N. Willow Rd., Schiller Park IL 60176. All rights reserved. Used with permission.

Page 63. "The Lord is my light." Music: James M. Burns. Text: ICEL. Copyright © 1970 World Library Publications, Inc., a division of J.S. Paluch Company, Inc., 3825 N. Willow Rd., Schiller Park IL 60176. All rights reserved. Used with permission.

Page 63. "If today." Music: David N. Johnson. Text: ICEL. Copyright © 1984 World Library Publications, Inc., a division of J.S. Paluch Company, Inc., 3825 N. Willow Rd., Schiller Park IL 60176. All rights reserved. Used with permission.

Page 63. "I will praise." Music: Howard Hughes, SM. Text: ICEL. Copyright © 1984 World Library Publications, Inc., a division of J.S. Paluch Company, Inc., 3825 N. Willow Rd., Schiller Park IL 60176. All rights reserved. Used with permission.

Page 68. "Lord, you raised." ICEL Resource Collection.

Page 70. "I know that my Redeemer lives." Music: Michael Dawney. ICEL Resource Collection.

Page 72. "I am the living bread." Music: Terrence Greaves. ICEL Resource Collection.

Page 97. "Cleanse us, O Lord." Music: Joseph Roff. Copyright © 1986 GIA Publications, Inc., Chicago. All rights reserved.